BFI WORKING PAPERS

NEW QUESTIONS OF
BRITISH CINEMA

Edited by Duncan Petrie

BFI PUBLISHING

First published in 1992 by the
British Film Institute
21 Stephen Street
London WIP IPL

Copyright © British Film Institute 1992

British Library Cataloguing in Publication Data

New Questions of British Cinema. – (BFI
Working Papers; v.2)
  I. Petrie, Duncan J. II. Series
  941.430941

ISBN 0–85170–322–4

Cover design by Roger Walton

Typeset in 10 on 11.5 Sabon by
Fakenham Photosetting Limited,
Fakenham, Norfolk
and printed in Great Britain by
St. Edmundsbury Press,
Bury St Edmunds, Suffolk

CONTENTS

BFI WORKING PAPERS

Working Papers represents a new publishing initiative from the British Film Institute's research division, intended to make theoretical and practical contributions to debate and reflect the BFI's current research activities and interests. Papers originate from both Institute staff and independent academics and journalists working closely with the BFI. Working Papers will bring together the writings and ideas of experienced commentators and critics while providing an important opportunity for new talent, the intention being to develop the latter source as the series progresses. Some volumes, such as this one, are intended to have a unifying theme while others will be more disparate and eclectic in content.

Most of this volume is derived from seminar papers presented at the BFI in late 1990 and early 1991.

NOTES ON CONTRIBUTORS

Duncan Petrie is a research officer in the Research Division of the BFI.

John Hill is senior lecturer in the Department of English, Media and Theatre Studies at the University of Ulster at Coleraine.

Colin MacCabe is head of the BFI Research Division.

Ben Gibson is head of BFI Production.

Richard Paterson is deputy head of the BFI Research Division.

James Mackay is an independent film producer.

Stephen Romer is a lecturer in economics at the Polytechnic of Central London.

Julian Petley is senior lecturer in the Department of Human Sciences at Brunel University.

James Roberts is a freelance writer and researcher.

Geoffrey Nowell-Smith is senior research fellow at the BFI and a freelance writer and lecturer.

INTRODUCTION

Duncan Petrie

The last major publication which subjected the structures and practices of the British film industry to critical examination was the collection *British Cinema Now*, edited by Nick Roddick and Martyn Auty
and published by the BFI in 1985. This book appeared at a time when
interest in the British cinema was high, fuelled by the media hype
surrounding the Oscar successes of *Chariots of Fire* and *Gandhi* in
successive years. This fervour was maintained in typically British style
by the self-promotional exercise of British Film Year in 1985. The
'British film revival' spawned several other books, including James
Park's *Learning to Dream: The New British Cinema*, John Walker's
The Once and Future Film, and *A Night at the Pictures: Ten Decades
of the British Film*, the official British Film Year publication edited by
Fenella Greenfield. Befitting the idea of the British cinema 'renaissance', these publications tended to be long on hyperbole and short on
substance and intelligent critique. As international interest in British
cinema began (inevitably) to wane, the euphoria dissipated and writers
turned their attentions to a more considered reappraisal and re-
interpretation of British cinema history and indigenous film-making
traditions.[1]

In contrast to the rather celebratory tone of most of the publications
noted above, recent writings on contemporary British cinema have
inclined to shift the focus on to issues of failure. James Park's brief
historical account *British Cinema: The Lights that Failed*, for
example, attempts to engage with what the author perceives as the
historical deficiencies of the British film industry (an interesting reappraisal of his own attitudes towards British cinema compared with
his earlier book). In a similar vein, Jake Eberts and Terry Illot's *My
Indecision is Final* is a mammoth in-depth analysis of the rise and fall
of Goldcrest Films, the company most associated with the British
'renaissance' and whose spectacular demise symbolically closed that
chapter of film-making history. My own book *Creativity and Constraint in the British Film Industry*, written in the late 80s and examin-

1

ing the film-making process in Britain, was initially conceived in an optimistic light, but as I worked through the history and industrial processes of British cinema certain fundamental problems, mainly of an economic nature, became more and more apparent.

While the concept of a 'renaissance' might have been an exaggeration, there was certainly a film-making revival generated largely by the decision of Channel 4 to invest substantially in low-budget British cinema, but its failure returned the historically maligned British film industry once again to rather dire straits. Production levels dipped to depressing lows, companies found survival increasingly difficult, and the lifeline provided by television finance which had been so important in the 80s began to look less secure. Such factors combined to create a climate where there is a very real sense that, unless some drastic action is taken, and taken quickly, we may not have a film industry to speak of left in this country. Some more cynical commentators, including one or two contributors to this volume, argue that we have reached this point already. By way of a depressing illustration, a report in *Screen International* of 19 April 1991 noted that there were only nine feature starts in the first quarter of 1991, and only two of these were fully British financed.

The primary objective of this volume is to identify and examine some of the problems currently facing the British film industry in an attempt to shed some welcome light on the structures of financing, production, distribution and marketing of British films and suggest how some of the current problems and structural weaknesses could be tackled. This collection is also intended to complement other recent BFI publications and research initiatives which explore the economics of the British film industry, in particular the *UK Film Initiatives* monograph series. These monographs represent the BFI's contribution to the ensuing debates about the problems faced by the industry generated in the wake of the Downing Street Seminar of June 1990. This series includes *The View from Downing Street* by Jane Headland and Simon Relph, an overview of the financial and structural problems of the industry; *The Need for Tax Incentives* (self-explanatory with regard to the argument it puts forward) by Michael Prescott; *Promoting the Industry* by Richard Lewis and Paul Marris, which emphasises the need for effective film distribution, sales and marketing, and makes the case for the setting up of a UK Film Commission; *Productive Relationships?* by Nick Smedley and John Woodward, which suggests how the relationships between the production sector and the structures of distribution and exhibition (including video and television) could be changed to rejuvenate British film-making; and *A Level Playing Field?* by Patricia Perilli, a report on the various fiscal and subsidy mechanisms supporting film production in continental Europe. While

2

these publications tend to take the form of policy documents setting out proposals to improve the current state of the British film industry, this volume is intended to be much more discursive, speculative, even polemical at times: a chance for contributors to 'think aloud' about the problems affecting the British film industry and what the way ahead might entail.

The British Film Industry in the 90s

British Cinema Now concluded with a provocatively entitled chapter 'But do we need it?' by Geoffrey Nowell-Smith which speculated on whether or not cinema had a future in British cultural life. The first essay in the present volume, by John Hill, is something of a reply to Nowell-Smith's question. Hill argues for the importance of a British 'national cinema', the cultural value of which could be analogous to the principle of public service broadcasting. However, he is also sensitive to the potentially reactionary undertones attached to arguments for a 'national cinema'. Hill suggests that such a cinema need not be narrowly nationalist in its concerns, but that it is possible to conceive of a national cinema which is nationally specific without being 'nationalist' nor attached to homogenising myths of a national identity. The classic example he cites is black British cinema, rooted in British cultural experience but sensitive to the real complexities of current British social and cultural configurations.

It is therefore worth interrogating what the 'British' in British cinema actually refers to. Hill's example of black British cinema raises the possibility of an acknowledgement of a diversity of cultural representations and identities within the rubric of 'British'. This in turn begs the question of whether we are talking about not one British cinema but several distinct cinematic identities. Even the concept of 'national' cinema in the case of Britain or the UK is problematic, given the mismatch of nation and state within these islands. Can reference be justifiably made to Scottish cinema, Welsh cinema or, indeed, Irish cinema (as well as the dominant English film-making tradition) as national cinemas in their own right? Certain developments over the past decade have suggested that, if we are talking in critical or cultural rather than economic terms, we should recognise such diverse currents as vital constituent parts of British cinema.

I would also wish to question the meaning of the second half of the concept British 'cinema'. It is impossible to talk about British film production from the early 80s onwards without also talking about British television. The absolutely crucial role played by Channel 4 in bankrolling the British film revival is commonly acknowledged. It was the production finance made available by commissioning editors such as David Rose and Alan Fountain which lay behind the resurgence in

3

British film-making in the early part of the decade, and which has effectively propped the industry up since then. As Nick Smedley and John Woodward bluntly put it, 'The 1980s effectively saw the British film industry starved, beaten senseless and plugged into a life-support system called Channel 4.'[4]

At one stage Channel 4 was contributing (in terms of both television presales and equity investments) to more than half of all the feature films produced in this country. They were also a major financial force behind British Screen and the BFI Production Board. Channel 4 contributed financially to most of the critical landmark films of the 80s, including *The Draughtsman's Contract, Angel, The Ploughman's Lunch, My Beautiful Laundrette, Caravaggio, Letter to Brezhnev, A Room With a View* and *Distant Voices, Still Lives.*

However, the significance of Channel 4 extends beyond the economic dimension. In an article referring specifically to film-making in Scotland, but having implications for the emergence of other cinematic identities within the UK, John Caughie argues that the importance of Channel 4 was not only in terms of its commissioning role, but crucially in its establishing a climate in which new forms of independent film production became viable and therefore fundable. The subsequent development and expansion generated in the independent production sector allowed greater access to the means of production to a much wider range of people, creating an unprecedented diversity in British audiovisual production: 'a diversity not only in forms of representation and in what, and who, can be represented, but also in the forms of production, and in the geographical and social locations from which it can come'.[3]

Channel 4 also enabled new voices to be heard nationwide, reflecting the diversity of the culture back at itself. Significantly, this could only be done in the 80s through the medium of television. As Caughie argues:

> Whatever the affection we may have for cinema, the capacity of television now to create not only representations but audiences for representations, is crucial to the development of a diverse culture: a national or regional culture as much as a film or television culture.[4]

This active participation in film production has been emulated to a greater or lesser degree by several of the ITV companies (most notably Granada) and, more recently, by the BBC. It is now difficult to find a film in the low- to medium-budget category which does not have television money as a crucial part of its financial package.

Hitherto, the major overseas investors in British cinema have been

North American distribution companies, which has (at least partly) left the fortunes of the British production industry in the hands of American executives who may or may not decide to continue investing in British product. The dramatic drop in the number of films produced in Britain in the late 80s was due in part to the withdrawal of American funds as several independent distributors, or 'mini-majors', who had been handling British films experienced economic problems and either cut back on investment or folded altogether. This rather precarious state of affairs has forced some British producers to explore alternative avenues for raising production finance. The obvious place to look in the 90s is continental Europe, and to the co-production possibilities afforded by various EC schemes and directives. Significantly, European co-production monies for British feature production have also tended to come from broadcasters such as ZDF in Germany and Le Sept in France, rather than cinema distributors.

The importance of both British television and the European dimension inform several of the contributions in this volume. Colin MacCabe's essay, for example, examines from a British perspective the question of funding European low-budget films. Low-budget cinema in Europe has generally been tied to forms of public subsidy, and the general conception is that, while the rest of Europe has demonstrated a financial and a cultural commitment to film-making through subsidy schemes, British cinema is impoverished precisely because it lacks such mechanisms. Against this popular notion, MacCabe argues that Channel 4 has effectively become the major element of subsidy (subsidy being a major component of European production) in British cinema, and furthermore, this structure of funding low-budget cinema is actually superior, in terms of the film-making process it facilitates, to systems of subsidy operating in continental Europe. This is primarily because such subsidy systems lead to the production of films which never consider the audience as part of the equation. MacCabe goes on to radically challenge the assumption that there is an essential difference between the production of films for the cinema and television.

Ben Gibson, currently head of BFI Production, notes the central role the BFI has found itself occupying, post-Downing Street, with regard to debates around the industry. He challenges various assumptions and received opinions informing these debates: the concept of a British film 'industry' itself, which he claims is actually 'a small service sector of the British television industry'; issues relating to the perception of 'subsidised' and 'commercial' film-making, in relation to the context of Europe; the differences between television and cinema films; the question of domestic and international audiences; the role of film schools; the benefits of stable studio production; and assumptions about what 'adequate' and 'necessary' budgetary levels and produc-

5

tion values are in British cinema. Gibson argues that the only way the industry can identify common interests, devise strategies and lobby government collectively in relation to policy decisions, is to interrogate rigorously such assumptions and orthodoxies. He also makes several interesting, and often polemical, suggestions as to the solution of some of the industry's major problems along the way.

While the bulk of the essays in this collection deal with questions of production they do not fix them in the same conceptual framework. In his analysis of the changing conditions of independent production in the UK, Richard Paterson brings to bear legal and economic discourse within the realm of the sociological. He critically examines developing relationships between independent producers and sources of finance by placing his focus on changing structures of governance, types of firm and contractual relationships. While Paterson considers independent production in relation to both television and cinema, his emphasis, unlike most of the other contributors, is very much on the former.

As Paterson points out, the emergence of Channel 4 and its commissioning approach to programme-making (including filmed drama) effectively generated the independent production sector in this country. This sector ranges from small independent producers who operate on a project-by-project basis to large fully capitalised concerns which have developed during the 80s and have in some cases now expanded into other sectors of the media. The current crisis has hit the smaller companies particularly hard but some continue to survive in the face of adversity. An interesting example of the experiences of one independent producer who has made films for both cinema and television is James Mackay. Mackay's credits as producer include three highly innovative features (in both aesthetic and technological terms) directed by Derek Jarman: *The Angelic Conversation, The Last of England* and *The Garden*. The major sources of finance for these have been television, both British and continental. Mackay's essay describes in detail the problems of realising such unorthodox production methods, and the uses of technology and narrative construction within a rather conservative and moribund industry.

The breadth of the British production sector is explored by Stephen Romer who examines different methods of raising finance and cost-control during a production, giving a sense of the existence of different 'types' (in an economic sense) of production within British feature film-making. Romer looks at five productions from the late 80s which range in budget from the £635,000 *Distant Voices, Still Lives*, funded by the British Film Institute and Channel 4, to the £4.5 million American-backed *A Fish Called Wanda*. This gives a more realistic account of the range of British production than Nick Roddick did in *British Cinema Now*, where the production sector was divided into three

6

'ideal types': commercial production, publicly subsidised production and television-funded production.[5]

It is more appropriate to make a distinction between different types of product in relation to the profile of their intended audience in all its forms: mass/specialist, mainstream/art house, domestic/international. The size of budgets in most cases reflect the project 'value' of any particular project in the market-place. It is better to think of films as either high, medium or low budget, with different sets of economic and cultural baggage attached to each, than as either commercial or subsidised. Part of the problem is a lack of an appropriately sophisticated concept of audiences and their preferences. The idea of the market-place is also not a straightforward one. Markets are segmented along various axes: by type of film, by country, by language, by type of market (theatrical, television, video), and so on. A major thrust of some of the later articles in this volume is structured around the question of improving ways in which British films can reach audiences and develop markets.

The problems faced by the production sector are closely linked to structural weaknesses in the distribution and exhibition sectors. Julian Petley suggests that the difficulties encountered by producers in finding a distribution outlet for their films compounds the problems of raising finance. Cinema distribution in Britain is dominated by a handful of large companies which handle almost exclusively mainstream Hollywood product. Such companies have a monopoly on cinema screens, making it extremely difficult for British or subtitled films to be effectively distributed and exhibited in this country. Those independent distributors which do handle such product face problems of limited exhibition outlets, and substantial costs of launching a new release in this country. Such factors combine to make it extremely difficult for independent distributors (particularly those without their own cinemas) to remain in business, let alone prosper – witness the demise of Oasis and Enterprise. Petley surveys various aspects of this problem and goes on to suggest possible solutions, including a British version of the EFDO scheme to encourage the distribution of low-budget films in the EC, or the possibility of a quota for independent distribution and exhibition, along the lines of the 25 per cent ruling imposed on British television.

To find an audience films need effective marketing. James Roberts argues that the film industry has essentially equated marketing with promotion and has consequently failed to recognise the potential benefits that could be delivered by adopting a broader view. He examines the practices of the film industry, contrasts them with the true scope of marketing, and suggests ways in which it could be better applied to British cinema. Particularly interesting is this essay's refusal to accept

7

the cultural value of cinema simply (which contributors such as Hill and Petley explicitly do) without considering the implications of questions of audience taste and commercial viability. British cinema has, Roberts argues, been effectively production and sales led and needs to adopt a more consumer-oriented approach. He asks the awkward question: even if we are able to produce more films in Britain and develop the mechanisms to distribute and exhibit them on a national and an international level, will people actually want to see them?

If questions of distribution and marketing are to be tackled, reliable and comprehensive information relating to the various markets for British films are required. Geoffrey Nowell-Smith's contribution to this volume highlights the very lack of such information. Nowell-Smith demonstrates the historical reasons for this dearth of rather straightforward trade information (leaving Britain the least well-informed country in Western Europe in terms of official statistics) and suggests the kind of economic statistics and general demographic information which should be provided. He focuses on the question of earnings of British films across *all* markets, and in particular the relations between gross and net earnings. Until such information is easily available, the kind of intelligent business decisions necessary to stabilise the British film industry, let alone enable it to thrive, cannot be taken with any degree of confidence.

Notes

1. Examples include Charles Barr (ed.), *All Our Yesterdays: 90 Years of British Cinema* (London: BFI, 1986), and Ian Christie's book on the films of Michael Powell and Emeric Pressburger, *Arrows of Desire* (London: Waterstone, 1985).
2. Nick Smedley and John Woodward, *Productive Relationships?*, UK Film Initiatives 4, (London: BFI, 1991).
3. John Caughie, 'Representing Scotland: New Questions For Scottish Cinema' in Eddie Dick (ed.), *From Limelight to Satellite* (London: BFI/SFC 1990), p. 23.
4. Caughie, 'Representing Scotland', p. 21.
5. Roddick constructs a model of British production consisting of three segments:
   (1) 'The commercial sector', which concerns product financed on the basis of a 'package', usually put together by a producer around a particular property: a subject, a director, a star. The commercial potential of this package is assessed on a one-off basis. The actual process of financing such a package is in terms of an initial presale to a major distributor (usually American), with the rest of the budget being raised on the open money market.

(2) 'The subsidised sector', covering more experimental and financially risky productions which will have difficulty in finding wide distribution. Films in this category are generally made on smaller budgets that those included in the commercial sector. The major sources of finance for subsidised films include the old NFFC, the BFI Production Board and regional arts associations (the workshop sector).

(3) 'The relationship between film and television': basically an acknowledgement of the involvement of Channel 4 in British film production.

Roddick implies that films tend to conform more or less to one of these types. His model is also underpinned by an assumption of the mutual exclusivity of the categories 'culture' and 'commerce'. Type (1) above refers to commercial production. The examples he gives are *The French Lieutenant's Woman*, *Never Say Never Again*, *Gandhi* and *Chariots of Fire*. The first three are international big-budget productions. Types (2) and (3), on the other hand, are effectively removed from the harsh realities of the market (Channel 4 representing a hidden subsidy) and allow greater cultural expression.

What this model does not reflect are those numerous productions (both at the time his article was written and since) which fit neither 'type' but rather combine finance from all three sectors identified by Roddick. For example, *A Room With a View* was produced with investments from Goldcrest and Curzon (both commercial companies), the NFFC and Channel 4. In fact, most of the features which received funding via the NFFC and its successor, British Screen, and Channel 4 have also been made with some degree of commercial interest. The importance of the less overtly commercial section of the budget is that a commitment from British Screen or Channel 4 (or both) can act as a lever to secure the remainder of a budget from, for example, a major distribution company. The pattern described has become more pronounced in recent years as funding partnerships become more and more complex. Clearly Roddick utilised 'ideal types' which are unable to account for the different patterns of investment and production in the British film industry.

THE ISSUE OF NATIONAL CINEMA AND BRITISH FILM PRODUCTION

John Hill

It is, perhaps, a symptom of the low esteem in which British cinema has traditionally been held that a book devoted to the prospects of British cinema in the 1980s should conclude with a chapter entitled, 'But do we need it?'[1] Although the article itself, by Geoffrey Nowell-Smith, was prompted by fears of the threat to the British cinema's survival, the fact that the question was posed in this way at all does suggest something of the lukewarm attitude towards British film that has often been prevalent among critics and, indeed, audiences. With the current low ebb in British film production, the shilly-shallying of the government in its policy towards the industry, and the decline in Channel 4's support for both feature production and workshop activities, the threat to the British cinema is now even greater than it was in the mid-80s. The importance of being able to argue successfully the case for why a national cinema is necessary or desirable has thus become all the more urgent. What I want to suggest, however, is that because of the lack of critical enthusiasm for the British cinema this is not always as easily accomplished at it might be and, indeed, that certain critical currents actually work against the case to be made.

To return to Geoffrey Nowell-Smith's question, there are two sets of arguments which are characteristically mobilised in defence of a national cinema. The first of these is economic and lays stress upon the value of a national film industry to the national economy in terms of the creation of jobs, attraction of overseas investment, export earnings and general knock-on effects for the service industries and tourism. Such arguments can become quite complex, both in terms of what counts as a specifically national cinema in an age of transnational communication industries and of how precisely the value of a film industry to the economy is to be measured. However, whatever the merits or otherwise of these arguments, they are fundamentally about the virtues of a national film *industry* rather than a national cinema proper, in the sense of a cinema that specifically attends to or addresses national concerns. It is, therefore, quite possible to conceive

10

of a British film industry, making films in Britain and employing British nationals, which is none the less not making recognisable British films. It is from this industrial standpoint that films like *Flash Gordon*, the *Superman* movies, *Insignificance* and *Full Metal Jacket* have qualified as 'British' films while, conversely, such a typically British film as *Shirley Valentine* is registered as American. This is not, of course, to say anything about the relative merits of these films but simply to note that economic arguments regarding the value of a national film industry do not necessarily guarantee a national cinema characterised by national preoccupations.

The case for a national cinema, then, is largely dependent upon cultural arguments. In particular, it is dependent upon a fundamental argument regarding the value of a home-grown cinema to the cultural life of a nation and, hence, the importance of supporting indigenous film-making in an international market dominated by Hollywood. However, such arguments are not straightforward and uncontested, and in the context of Britain the value of a 'British national cinema', both in itself and as a bulwark against Hollywood, has often been questioned. Such questions are, of course, linked to critical debates regarding the relative artistic merits of British and Hollywood films but have also been fuelled by more general intellectual trends: in particular, a growing scepticism towards and critical scrutiny of traditional conceptions of the nation, national identity and nationalism, and an increasing emphasis, within media studies, on the moment of reception and the active role played by media audiences. I want, therefore, to examine briefly these intellectual trends and assess their consequences for arguments in favour of a British national cinema. Although they would appear to work against such arguments I want to suggest that this need not neccesarily be the case, and that it is still desirable to argue for the importance of a British cinema, albeit on grounds which may differ from the conventional.

It has been argued by Richard Collins that many of the theoretical presuppositions of media and film studies in the 70s no longer hold sway. In particular, he argues that the 'dominant paradigm' of media studies – what he refers to, after Abercrombie et al., as 'the dominant ideology thesis' – has been subject to considerable strain.[2] While it could be argued that Collins (like Abercrombie and his colleagues) attributes far too neat a coherence to the various versions of the 'dominant ideology thesis', it is undoubtedly the case that enthusiasm for ideology critique has waned substantially. Three main reasons for this may be identified. First, there has been a querying and reformulation of the theories of ideology themselves. In particular, there has been a questioning both of the existence of a set of coherent and internally consistent ideas, values and attitudes that could actually be

11

identified as the 'dominant ideology' and of the importance of ideology (as opposed to economic constraint and pragmatism) in the winning of political consent and securing of social cohesion. Secondly, at the level of textual analysis, there has been a growing emphasis on the polysemy of media texts, the plurality (as opposed to singularity) of the meanings which texts may be seen to encourage, and on the potential ideological tensions and contradictions which may result. Finally, and for the purpose of this paper perhaps most importantly, there has been a growing emphasis on the role of audiences. Whereas 70s film theory was characterised by an emphasis upon the analysis of a film's textual operations and the spectator position which these encouraged, an increasing tendency within media studies during the 80s was empirically based audience research and a theoretical stress on the ability of audiences actively to construct their own readings of, and impose their own meanings upon, media texts.[3] Thus, if earlier film and media theory appeared to assume that audience response (or 'ideological effect') could simply be read off the text (or accounted for in psychoanalytic terms which were difficult to assess empirically) more recent media theory has tended to downplay the importance of the actual characteristics of texts in favour of an emphasis upon the interpretative licence and creativity enjoyed by media audiences.

While this development has provided a corrective to the 'textual determinism' of 70s (and, indeed, much contemporary) film theory, it has also directed attention away from questions of the ownership and control of the media and the ways in which these relations may be seen to curtail the range and diversity of media forms and representations.[4] Indeed, an emphasis on the 'power' of audiences tends not only to discourage an interest in these issues but also to encourage a more ready acceptance of current media output and so lessen the demand for alternative, or simply different, types of films and television programmes. There is a clear difference, in this respect, from those perspectives which such work is superseding. Criticism of texts on ideological grounds, for example, was motivated in part by a belief that it was possible to envisage media work which did not display such shortcomings. In the same way, 70s film theory, whatever the merits of its commitment to avant-garde aesthetics, was closely identified with support for and promotion of new forms of film-making practice. For the newer kinds of reception theory, however, the relative freedom of the audience to produce its own meanings in relation to texts makes the encouragement of new types of media practice much less a priority. Indeed, in a curious inversion of the old orthodoxy, John Fiske comes close to arguing for not only the acceptability but also the desirability of ideologically conservative films such as *Rambo* on the grounds that they provide material for audiences actively to resist.[5]

12

If this dilution of the 'dominant ideology thesis' in media studies and the corresponding emphasis on the activity of audiences may be seen to have weakened the case for new and alternative forms of media production, much the same could also be said in respect of the case for a national cinema. Indeed, to take the example of John Fiske once more, it can be seen how his audience-oriented approach is used to argue against the need for 'special-interest' or culturally specific work on the grounds that 'diversity' does not depend upon the actual range of media output which is available but is, for him, 'audience-pro-duced'.[6]

This is, of course, an argument which would also apply in respect of British cinema, and something of a similar drift may be detected in recent writing on British audiences' response to Hollywood films. As Nowell-Smith suggests, 'the hidden history of cinema in British cul-ture, and in popular culture in particular, has been the history of American films popular with the British public'.[7] In seeking to analyse the popularity of American films with British working-class audiences in particular, Nowell-Smith and others have put into question conven-tional assumptions about the 'dangers' – either to cultural standards or national identity – which Hollywood's domination of British screens has been alleged to present. Hollywood films, from this point of view, may be seen to offer pleasures, attitudes and meanings not to be found in either British films or British culture more generally, and which may be appropriated and made use of by British audiences in culturally specific ways. It is on this basis that Tony Bennett is able to argue that the impact of American popular culture, including film, in Britain has been 'positive' in 'making available a repertoire of cultural styles and resources ... which, in various ways, have undercut and been consciously mobilised against the cultural hegemony of Britain's traditional elites'.[8]

While this is an argument that is undoubtedly accurate, there are dangers, none the less, in what conclusions are drawn from it. For just as the emphasis in media studies more generally on the polysemy of texts and the activity of audiences has tended towards a legitimisation of existing relations and practices of media production and distri-bution, so an emphasis on the progressive qualities of Hollywood films for British audiences may serve to ratify existing relations of film production and undermine the case for a specifically British cinema.[9]

This may be illustrated by an article on national cinema by Andrew Higson. In line with current trends in audience study, Higson suggests that 'the parameters of a national cinema should be drawn at the site of consumption as much as the site of production of films' and, thus, include 'the activity of national audiences and the conditions under

13

which they make sense of and use the films they watch'.[10] The problem with this formulation, however, is that it appears to lead to the conclusion that Hollywood films are in fact a part of the British national cinema because these are the films which are primarily used and consumed by British national audiences. Clearly Hollywood films do play a major role within British film culture. However, to elide the distinction, as Higson does, between the *cinema in Britain* and British *national cinema* seems not only to be conceptually unhelpful but also, by virtue of the emphasis on *consumption*, to blur the arguments for film *production* which is specifically British rather than North American.

What, of course, adds to this problem is that arguments regarding film consumption and the positive aspects of US films in a British context are often linked to a certain disdain for the conventional characteristics of British films. As Nowell-Smith suggests, when compared with their American counterparts, British films have often come across as 'restrictive and stifling, subservient to middle-class artistic models and to middle- and upper-class values'.[11] The continuing preoccupation of 'quality' British cinema with literary adaptation, the past, and the lives and loves of the upper classes also suggests that Nowell-Smith's remarks retain their relevance. However, they cannot be seen to apply uniformly, and certainly fail to do justice to the more varied forms and representations which have been a feature of British film-making in the 80s. Nevertheless, even if Nowell-Smith's remarks were entirely justified it would still be important to defend the *principle* of a national British cinema even if current practice was less than could be wished for. The argument, in this respect, may be viewed as analogous to that regarding the concept of public service broadcasting. While historically the actual practice of public service broadcasting may have had its shortcomings, the principles which have underlain it still remain worth defending (especially when, as at present, under attack).[12]

What is at stake here, however, is not simply the artistic merits of British films but also the versions of national identity which they have conventionally provided. Criticism of the British cinema, in this regard, is often associated with a more general critique of the traditional conceptions of nationalism and national identity with which British films have characteristically been linked. As Raphael Samuel has argued, 'nationality no longer belongs to the realm of the taken-for-granted', and conventional conceptions of the nation, nationalism, national identity and national culture have all been subject to critical scrutiny in recent writings.[13] At the risk of simplification, the main lines of argument may be identified.

First, it has been argued that while nation-states undoubtedly exist

14

and play a substantial role in the shaping of economic, political and cultural realities, nations and national identities as such are not onto-logically given but represent 'imagined' or socially and culturally con-structed communities and forms of belonging.[14] From this basic insight it follows that national identity and the cultural forms in which it is given expression must be conceived of in dynamic, or what Philip Schlesinger has referred to as 'actionist', terms.[15] This has three main consequences for the conception of national cultures and the ways in which they construct national identities. First, these must be seen not to be fixed and static but subject to historical change, redefinition and even 'reinvention'. Second, they cannot be regarded as straightfor-wardly 'pure' and bounded but rather as hybrid and in interaction with 'outside' cultural influences and identities. Third, they cannot be conceived of as unproblematically unified or as the automatic ex-pression of different social groups within the 'nation', but rather as sites of actual and potential contestation and challenge.

Hence, it is a constant criticism of nationalism that it seeks to impose upon the nation not only a historically frozen and hermetically sealed (or 'authentic') conception of identity but also an imaginary sense of unity which fails to take account of the variety of collective identities and forms of belonging (such as class, gender, ethnicity and region) which may exist within the national community. In the case of Britain this suppression of difference is all the greater in so far as there is more than one national community within the boundaries of the nation-state and, therefore, no obvious alignment between 'national culture' and nation-state of the sort assumed by nationalist ideology. Thus, the resurgence of nationalist sentiment (and concern for national sovereignty) characteristic of the Thatcher years has been pre-eminently an *English* nationalism to which the claims to 'national identity' of Scotland and Wales (along with various other forms of collective identity) have been subordinated.

To return to the earlier argument, it can now be seen why such arguments are unsympathetic to the case for a national cinema, imply-ing, as they do, that such a cinema will either be narrowly nationalist or else in hock to a restricted or homogenising view of national ident-ity. It also provides a further reason for the enthusiasm of critics and writers for American rather than British films in so far as, as one observer puts it, 'the heterogeneity of "the popular"' as presented by Hollywood may be seen to challenge 'the fixity of the "national"' as exemplified by British cinema and British culture more generally.[16]

However, while it is certainly the case that British films have often depended upon and promoted quite restricted notions of national identity, what I want to suggest is that the idea of a national cinema in itself does not necessarily imply this sense of 'fixity'. It is true, none the

15

less, that national cinema has often been conceptualised in this way. This can be seen from two examples. Writing in the context of Australian cinema, Susan Dermody and Elizabeth Jacka, drawing on the work of John Hinde, suggest that 'the *true* national cinema' (my italics) is characterised by a strong bond or 'feedback loop' between films and audiences.[17] In a similar fashion, Raphael Samuel suggests that in comparison with other periods, British cinema in the 40s *was* 'national cinema', and thus provides 'a precious index to the imaginative preoccupations of the time'.[18] In both cases, the idea employed of a natural cinema implies a tight, symbiotic relation between films and audiences and a clear, unified version of national identity and national preoccupations. At an empirical level, this is probably a more problematic phenomenon than the writers suggest. In the case of wartime Britain, for example, both the unity of the national community and the inclusiveness of the representations of national identity provided by the cinema may be queried.[19] Whatever the empirical evidence, however, it does not seem necessary or, indeed, desirable that national cinema (to be regarded as properly national) be required to conform to these characteristics. What I want to argue instead is that it is quite possible to conceive of a national cinema which is *nationally specific* without being either nationalist or attached to homogenising myths of national identity. One of the weaknesses of Andrew Higson's formulations, in this respect, is that, in dealing with the idea of a national cinema, he simply runs together 'national specificity' with 'imaginary coherence' and 'a unique and stable identity'.[20]

However, as Paul Willemen has argued, 'the discourses of nationalism and those addressing or comprising national specificity are not identical'.[21] To illustrate this point he takes the example of the black British films of the 80s, which he argues are 'strikingly British' without being nationalistic. Indeed, what is noticeable about such films, be it *My Beautiful Laundrette* or *Passion of Remembrance*, is not only the expanded sense of 'Britishness' which they offer but also their sensitivity to social differences (of ethnicity, class, gender and sexual orientation) within an identifiably and specifically British context. From this point of view, it is quite possible to conceive of a national cinema, in the sense of one which works with or addresses nationally specific materials, which is none the less critical of inherited notions of national identity, which does not assume the existence of a unique or unchanging 'national culture', and which is quite capable of dealing with social divisions and differences. Indeed, in a provocative reversal of the usual criteria for a 'national cinema', Willemen argues that the 'genuinely' national cinema can, in fact, be neither nationalist nor homogenising in its assumptions about national identity if it is to address successfully the complexities of nationally specific social and cultural configurations. Thus, arguments which in one light appear to undermine the case for a national cinema may be seen in this light to make its existence all the more important and pressing.

The difficulty, of course, is that a nationally specific cinema characterised by questioning and inquiry is not the kind of 'national cinema' which is encouraged by the market-place. This is not simply because success in the international market requires the downplaying of national specificity in favour of a spurious 'universal' appeal. As Thomas Elsaesser has argued, the employment of 'nationally specific', but none the less 'internationally recognisable', referents in films can be of critical importance to the marketing and international success of a film.[22] Rather, the problem is that the marketing of national specificity for international consumption is likely to encourage the use of the most conventional or readily recognisable markers of nationality and national identity. Hence, as Elsaesser observes, 'British films ... have been rather successful in marketing and packaging the national literary heritage, the war years, the countryside, the upper classes and élite education', and, in doing so, have also succeeded in constructing and circulating quite limiting and restricted versions of 'Britishness'.[23] Thus, the images of Britain where are most readily exportable are precisely those which a more enquiring (or 'proper') national cinema would seek to challenge.

It is for this reason that Willemen argues that a national cinema of the kind he envisages is characteristically a 'poor' and a 'dependent' cinema. It is also a further reason why cultural rather than economic arguments are the most important ones for the defence of national cinema. Not only is a British cinema left simply to the mercy of market forces unlikely to flourish (or, indeed, survive), but the type of British film which is most able to exploit international economic opportunities is not necessarily of the type most capable of making a valuable contribution to British cultural life.

It has to be recognised, of course, that such a perspective is at odds with the premises on which recent (and not so recent) government film policy has been based. As the sole White Paper on film to appear in the 80s, *Film Policy* (1984), makes apparent, British cinema has been regarded by government as straightforwardly a 'commercial film industry'.[24] The case for support for the British cinema on either 'artistic' or 'public service' grounds is simply not acknowledged. Indeed, the only 'cultural' argument to appear anywhere in the White Paper concerns 'national pride' and the value to the 'country's international standing' of British films which advertise 'the national culture and way of life to a wide audience overseas'.[25] Apart from drawing upon an entirely problematic conception of 'the (sic) national culture', this argument pays no attention at all to the contribution of British

17

films to cultural debate and understanding *inside* Britain and the value which might be attached to this.

Given the nature of the economic policies pursued by the Conservative government in recent years and the accompanying hostility to 'subsidy', it has been tempting for those arguing in support of a British cinema to abandon cultural arguments in favour of 'hard-headed' economic ones (or, as James Park has recently done, propound a blunt 'commonsense' of the sort that the money is available if only British producers could demonstrate the correct mix of 'energy, imagination' and 'sound business sense').[26] While such arguments may have some tactical merit, it seems to me that in the long term they are unlikely to ensure the continuing viability of a British cinema or deliver the infrastructure which it will require. As Elsaesser has argued, in the context of the 'new German cinema', a flourishing national cinema is dependent upon a 'politics of culture' or cultural commitment to the political support of film which is itself born of 'a will to create and preserve a national film and media ecology amidst an ever-expanding international film, media and information economy'.[27]

Clearly no such will currently exists in British political circles. However, in a sense, this makes the insistence upon the cultural dimension of film production all the more important, as it is only on the basis of a renewed cultural and political commitment to national film 'ecology' that British cinema is likely to prosper. To return to my opening remarks, this is also why it is important that arguments for a national cinema should be supported. Although motivated by 'progressive' cultural impulses, the combination of critical suspicion of the 'national' and populist celebrations of audience preferences may simply end up endorsing the operations of the market place (and its domination by transnational conglomerates) and, hence, the restricted range of cultural representations which the market provides. The case for a national cinema, in this respect, may be seen as part of a broader case for a more varied and representative range of film and media output than the current political economy of the communications industries allows.

I began by citing Geoffrey Nowell-Smith's question regarding the British cinema: do we need it? On strict utilitarian grounds, it would have to be conceded that the British cinema does not constitute a basic necessity. However, even though we might not need it, we might legitimately *want* the British cinema to survive and flourish. If we do, and basically I have argued that we should, then it becomes a question of what *kind* of British cinema we want. The implication of my argument is that the most interesting type of British cinema, and the one which is most worthy of support, differs from the type which is often hoped for – a British cinema capable of competing with Hollywood

18

and exemplifying the virtues and values of Britain. A different conception of British cinema recognises that its economic ambitions will have
to be more modest. However, its cultural ambitions can, and should,
be correspondingly more ambitious: the provision of diverse and challenging representations adequate to the complexities of contemporary
Britain.

Notes

This is a revised version of a paper originally delivered to the International
Communication Association Annual Conference, Dublin, 1990.

1. Geoffrey Nowell-Smith, 'But do we need it?', in Nick Roddick and Martin
   Auty (eds), *British Cinema Now* (London: British Film Institute, 1985).
2. Richard Collins, 'Paradigm Lost?', in his *Television: Policy and Culture*
   (London: Unwin Hyman, 1990). See also Nicholas Abercrombie, Stephen
   Hill and Bryan S. Turner, *The Dominant Ideology Thesis* (London: Allen
   and Unwin, 1984). For the sake of convenience I am accepting Collins's
   lumping together of film and media studies, although I am conscious that
   their intellectual trajectories have been distinctive. For an example of the
   difficulties in accommodating film studies within mainstream media
   research, see James Curran, 'The New Revionism in Mass Communication Research: A Reappraisal', *European Journal of Communication*,
   vol. 15, nos 2–3, 1990.
3. For a recent selection of essays within this tradition, see Ellen Seiter et al.,
   Remote Control Television Audiences and Cultural Power (London:
   Routledge, 1989).
4. David Morley has recently responded to criticisms of this type by arguing
   that the objective of audience research should not be to substitute micro-
   for macro-analysis but rather 'to integrate the analysis of the "broader
   questions" of ideology, power and politics ... with the analysis of the
   consumption, uses and functions of television in everyday life'. However,
   his subsequent formulation that this will lead to 'the production of
   analyses of the specific relationships of particular audiences to the particular types of media content which are located within the broader framework of an analysis of media consumption and domestic ritual' still seems
   to put to the side questions of media ownership and control. See 'Where
   the global meets the local: notes from the sitting room', *Screen*, vol. 32,
   no. 1, Spring 1991, p. 5.
5. John Fiske, *Understanding Popular Culture* (Boston: Unwin Hyman,
   1989), p. 57.
6. John Fiske, *Television Culture* (London: Methuen, 1987), p. 320
7. Nowell-Smith, 'But do we need it?', pp. 151–2.
8. Tony Bennett, 'Popular Culture and Hegemony in post-war Britain', in
   Politics, Ideology and Popular Culture (1) (Milton Keynes: Open University Press, 1982), p. 13.
9. In an analogous case, Stuart Cunningham discusses how cultural studies'
   privileging of the active audience was used by John Docker to argue

19

against Australian content regulation for television. See 'Cultural theory and broadcasting policy: some Australian observations', *Screen*, vol. 32, no. 1, Spring 1991. Cunningham's recommendation that 'cultural theory ... must take greater stock of its potential negative influence on progressive public policy outcomes' (ibid., p. 85) is clearly salient to my own argument. Jostein Gripsrud, commenting on the link between macro and micro issues in audience studies, has also stressed the importance of theory in 'the production of ideas about *alternatives* to given conditions' and, hence, its role in guiding what empirical questions are attended to in the first place. See, 'Notes on the Role of Theory', paper delivered to the International Communication Association Annual Conference, Dublin, 1990.

10. Andrew Higson, 'The Concept of National Cinema', *Screen*, vol. 30, no. 4, Autumn 1989, p. 36.
11. Nowell-Smith, 'But do we need it?', p. 152.
12. For a similar argument, see Paddy Scannell, 'Public Service Broadcasting: The History of a Concept', in Andrew Goodwin and Garry Whannel (eds), *Understanding Television* (London: Routledge, 1990). John Caughie suggests a comparison between public service broadcasting and 'public service cinema' in 'Broadcasting and Cinema: 1 – Converging Histories', in Charles Barr (ed.), *All Our Yesterdays: 90 Years of British Cinema* (London: British Film Institute, 1986).
13. Raphael Samuel, 'Introduction: Exciting to be English', in R. Samuel (ed.), *Patriotism: The Making and Unmaking of British National Identity*, vol. 1, *History and Politics* (London: Routledge, 1989), p. xix.
14. The classic statement of this position may be found in Benedict Anderson, *Imagined Communities: Reflections on the Origin and Spread of Nationalism* (London: Verso, 1983). For a more recent discussion see Homi K. Bhaba (ed.), *Nation and Narration* (London: Routledge, 1990).
15. Philip Schlesinger, 'On National Identity: some conceptions and misconceptions criticized', *Social Science Information*, vol. 26, no. 2, 1987, p. 260.
16. James Donald, 'How English Is It? Popular Literature and National Culture', *New Formations*, no. 6, Winter 1988, p. 33.
17. Susan Dermody and Elizabeth Jacka, *The Screening of Australia*, vol. 1, *Anatomy of a Film Industry* (Sydney: Currency Press, 1987), p. 34.
18. Raphael Samuel, 'Introduction: Exciting to be English', p. xxviii.
19. See, for example, Graham Dawson and Bob West, 'Our Finest Hour? The Popular Memory of World War II and the Struggle Over National Identity', in Geoff Hurd (ed.), *National Fictions* (London: British Film Institute, 1984); also Jeffrey Richards, 'National Identity in British Wartime Films', in Philip Taylor (ed.) *Britain and the Cinema in the Second World War* (Basingstoke: Macmillan, 1989).
20. Andrew Higson, 'The Concept of National Cinema', pp. 37–8.
21. Paul Willemen, 'The National', Paper delivered to International Communication Association Annual Conference, Dublin, 1990. I am grateful to Paul Willemen for making this paper available to me.
22. Thomas Elsaesser, *New German Cinema: A History* (Basingstoke: Macmillan/BFI, 1989), p. 322.
23. Thomas Elsaesser, 'Images for England (and Scotland, Ireland, Wales ...)',

Monthly Film Bulletin, September 1984, p. 208. For a comparable analysis of how Australian attempts to compete in the international market have led to films which 'blur social and economic processes behind notions of the nation, of Australianness, of the Australian character and the Australian people', see Sam Rhodie, 'The Film Industry', in Ted Wheelwright and Ken Buckley (eds), *Communications and the Media in Australia* (Sydney: Allen and Unwin, 1987), p. 155.

24. *Film Policy*, Cmnd 9319, (London: HMSO, 1984), p. 1. The 1985 Films Act which followed this White Paper abolished the Cinematograph Films Council, ended the Eady levy on exhibitors and 'privatised' the National Film Finance Corporation. Although notable for the extent of its hostility towards state support for film, the document does conform, none the less, to a long-standing tradition of film policy and legislation which, as Margaret Dickinson and Sarah Street have argued, has been conceived within 'the framework of commercial policy'. See *Cinema and State: The Film Industry and the British Government 1927–84* (London: British Film Institute, 1985).

25. *Film Policy*, p. 18.

26. James Park, *British Cinema: The Lights that Failed* (London: Batsford, 1990), p. 168. Less hard-headed, however, is Park's rather bizarre recommendation for the establishment of 'script factories' (ibid., p. 173). His enthusiasm for the enterprise of producers also ignores John Caughie's point that 'the centrality of producers to British cinema' (such as Dean, Korda, Balcon, Grierson, Puttnam) has, in fact, been a consequence of the absence in Britain of either 'a stable industrial infrastructure' or 'consistent public support' for the cinema. See Caughie's 'Representing Scotland: New Questions for Scottish Cinema' in Eddie Dick (ed.), *From Limelight to Satellite: A Scottish Film Book* (London: BFI/SFC, 1990), p. 22.

27. Thomas Elsaesser, *New German Cinema*. p. 3.

SUBSIDIES, AUDIENCES, PRODUCERS

Colin MacCabe

It is true that the direct amount of government subsidy to film production in Western European countries is much greater than in Britain. Indeed, the comparative figures are almost comical in their disproportion. For example, the city of Hamburg enjoys a film subsidy three times greater than the whole of Britain. Usually when these figures are cited it is to indicate just how bad things are in Britain and, conversely, how wonderful European cinema is in comparison. What this argument often ignores, however, is the fact that the vast majority of these subsidised European films are never seen by anybody at all. Consequently, the argument I want to deploy in this paper is the apparently perverse one that the structure which evolved for funding low-budget British films in the 80s was much better than its Continental equivalents, and that if we are serious about European film in the 90s then it is Britain that will need to be taken as a model.

The crucial financial and administrative element in British films in the 80s was Channel 4. When Jeremy Isaacs made his application to be Chief Executive of the new channel, he made clear his intention to take some 10 per cent of its revenues and devote them to reviving British cinema. The immediate result was that some £10 million a year suddenly became available for film production. Because Channel 4 is a limited company nobody ever describes this as a subsidy, but it is perhaps best understood as a parafiscal levy on British television revenues. Therefore, there was actually more subsidy money available in Britain during that decade than any account of government support would acknowledge. The influence of Channel 4, however, was not simply as a provider of funds. Precisely because the money was not an official subsidy, it was dispensed very differently from a normal subsidy, and such differences, I would argue, were crucial to the success of British cinema in the mid-80s.

The first and most striking difference between Channel 4 and a conventional film subsidy is the decision-making procedure employed. In the case of the majority of subsidies, decisions are taken by a board

22

or panel to which the administrative officer of the fund reports. Channel 4's decisions, on the other hand, were taken by an individual commissioning editor. The system by which projects are selected by a board, which is held to represent a variety of interests,[1] is one which determines that choices are made in relation to the various constituencies which feel they have some claim on the fund. Choices are made as a set of political brokerings on the board so that every interest feels that it has had its just reward. In this context, very little thought is actually given to the film's ultimate reception; members of the board feel they have fulfilled their task when they have successfully fought for their constituency. Crucially, nobody has a real stake in the film's success either critically or commercially.

The argument is not simply one of the virtues of the individual over the collective but rather about the way in which, if one person is held responsible for a set of funding decisions, then it is much easier for him or her to appeal to the reception of the films as justification for these decisions. Immediately a film's audience, however conceived, begins to figure in the decisions to produce, the more likely it becomes that some effort will be made to reach that audience. At the same time, one must recognise the political and bureaucratic reality which is the reluctance to hand over control of public money to a single individual for an unlimited period of time. This particular circle can be squared very easily by making all such appointments for a fixed period of time, and for continuing with the use of a board but with retrospective and watchdog rather than executive powers.

The second striking feature of Channel 4's input into film-making was just how central producers were to the whole process. Few accounts of the *nouvelle vague* or neo-realism stress the contribution of producers, but any account of British cinema in the 80s needs to ascribe as much significance to companies like Palace and Working Title as to individual directors like Stephen Frears or Neil Jordan. In one sense this may simply be explained by the structure of financing in the 80s. The complicated funding of many of those films which linked British television money with distribution advances from American independents ensured a major role for whoever could tie the funding together. At the same time it is interesting to reflect that this gave producers an importance which they do not enjoy in European countries.

The knee-jerk reaction of the culturally correct is that the European disregard for the producer is obviously a good thing; indeed, it simply proves the superiority of European cinema. One could argue, however, that if the producer is denied any role whatsoever (and the legislation governing film production in France and Germany would seem to deprive the producer of any power), then inevitably one will see films made which have little or no regard for their audience. There is no question that *Cahiers*'s emphasis on the director was a much-needed historical corrective. Indeed, my own experience of production has absolutely convinced me of the central role of the director as the key person who orchestrates the variety of creative inputs which go to make up a finished film. However, it does not follow that this means that the director should have absolute control of the process. Undoubtedly, one of the problems is the very dominant role allocated to the director in most low-budget European film-making.

The problem with this dominance is exactly that it is all too likely to lead to a complete disregard of the audience. The time and effort that Hollywood puts into the redrafting of scripts and the editing of films are the visible signs of how the audience is always in play during the process of making a film, in a way in which they are not in our dominant models of artistic and literary production. It is this fact which makes the writer-director who entirely controls the process from beginning to end the exception (not to say the anomaly) rather than the rule. It is true that there are directors who work successfully while enjoying total control, but it is rare to find an individual who can simultaneously immerse him or herself in the complex details of film-making while also having a detached critical viewpoint (an approximation of that of the audience). This detached view needs to be provided by the producer. What was striking about the subsidy system that was effectively set up in Britain in the 80s was that it allowed producers a role which, while normally allowing the director the final say, forced him or her to listen to the arguments being carried on around them, thus bringing a consideration of the audience into the process of production.

Before developing my argument about the way in which subsidies should be structured I want to make a detour to consider some of Ben Gibson's arguments in his contribution to this volume.[2] While I tend to agree with almost all of what he says in terms of the steps needed to help independent low-budget production in Britain, I fundamentally disagree with two of his basic assumptions. Firstly, the idea that European films are evidently superior to their British counterparts simply ignores the fact that many young European film-makers during the 80s saw the situation as entirely the reverse. Secondly, and more crucially, I would like to take issue with the attempt to propose a Manichean division between film and television which I find more damaging, both intellectually and politically.

Before I attempt to consider the intellectual arguments about film and television I must confess that I have an enormous gut prejudice in favour of British television as opposed to British cinema. Until the 80s it was always British television rather than British film to which I

24

looked to for ideas and entertainment. Indeed, it has always seemed to me that the revival of British cinema in that decade can be (rather crudely) described in terms of a transfer of talent out of television and into cinema. Therefore I have little initial sympathy with any argument which simply and essentially posits film as a superior medium to television.

There are two obvious ways to compare film and television: the forms of production and the forms of reception. If one considers Britain, and indeed Europe, today one might be tempted to make the claim that film was less bureaucratic than television. The reason for this is that film is, by and large, organised on the basis of individual productions while television is organised as a continuous production. It is this difference which would seem to make film much less bureaucratic; as very few working relations last for more than the length of the production there is an impression of much more fluidity and less rigidity in film. I would not wish to deny this difference, which can be best described as the difference between a form of production which can be compared to the establishment and dismantling of a small-scale factory, and a form of production which resembles the continuous production of goods from a medium-sized factory.

However, while I would not wish to deny that this distinction is important, it does not constitute an *essential* difference between film and television. You only have to consider the way in which the Hollywood studio system functioned in its heyday, or the current development of television in Britain from in-house to independent production, to realise that there is nothing essential which divides film and television into different kinds of production units. Current British film production benefits from the creative advantages of small-scale and continuously renewed production units – namely, the possibility of experimentation, change and novelty. On the other hand, this state of affairs also entails certain creative disadvantages such as a lack of stability and the consequent inability to guarantee levels of quality or to gradually develop new areas of expertise. These advantages and disadvantages are, however, historically contingent – they are not essential to film, as opposed to television.

If we turn to the question of modes of reception, then there is no doubt that there are fundamental differences between film and television. Firstly, one has a different physical relation to the image. In the cinema one sits in a darkened room in which considerable effort is made to ensure that your entire sensory field is dominated by an image much larger than your body. Television, on the other hand, offers us an image much smaller than our bodies in the context of the whole range of alternative stimuli. Secondly, this physical distinction underpins the radically different ways in which we are addressed socially by

25

film and television. Although we go to the cinema in a group, the conditions of viewing mean that we see films as isolated individuals. Television, on the other hand, even if we watch it alone at home, addresses us as members of an implied wider audience. I think that it is probably difficult to underestimate how little we know about these distinctions and how important they are. One might hazard a guess that it is film's physical situation that brings it so much closer to a dream state than television, and it seems equally clear that television is continuously addressing us as citizens. However, to develop these insights and to test them within a general theory of the image is impossible at this stage, given our so inadequate state of knowledge.

Despite these huge differences in the conditions of reception, I still remain very sceptical of those who wish to construct on that basis an essential opposition between film and television. Crudely put, if you take any work of fiction made for television which you consider to have any merit and project it cinematically, it will gain a certain force in that projection. Indeed, that assumption is what lies behind the increasingly successful television festival run each January in Cannes. Conversely, almost any film which works in the cinema will also function on television.[3]

My point therefore is not to deny the differences between film and television, but to deny any *absolute* oppositions or hierarchies. One is then, however, faced with the problem that such absolutes are meat and drink to some film-makers and, more importantly, they are the foundation of many of the discourses which surround discussions of cinema funding in Europe. In fact, within these discourses, television is simply an unquestioned term of contempt.

Much of this is explicable by the recognition of a simple snobbery which relies on the cinema's claim to a certain kind of élite status which renders it, and its devotees, superior to the *hoi-polloi* of television. If we ignore this snobbery we can perhaps discern an argument about form lurking in this appeal to pure cinema. One of the great modernist arguments which has reverberated through the twentieth century is the appeal to the purity of form. According to such an account, art is essentially concerned with neither content nor audience but rather with its own structures and procedures.

Ironically enough, this kind of argument is one which finds much of its force in opposition to the new media of the twentieth century, and there is something truly uncanny hearing it applied to cinema itself. When Mallarmé sits down to write the book to come, the book is written for a future audience which will appreciate its complete devotion to the symbol. He does so to avoid the ever-burgeoning current audiences which devour the popular entertainment of the day, from the yellow press to the music hall. Modernist literature finds

26

much of its force in a crisis of the national audience precipitated by the growth of literacy and of new popular forms. But literature, like the other traditional arts, can at least pretend to have an existence independent of an audience. Indeed, one of the still dominant images of the writer, the Romantic artist starving in his garret, depends for its force on the reality of the writer's art independently of its reception.

On the other hand, the very structure of a film's production involves an audience and it is, therefore, extraordinary to find essentialist accounts which attempt to describe cinema without embracing the continuous construction of an audience. I am not arguing that this audience is simple, homogeneous or unified, but merely that one cannot think of film outside the possibility of projection, which immediately implies an audience (even if only its makers) for whom the film is being projected. In these terms, any argument about the essentiality of form, which implies that art can be discussed independently of its audience, is deeply misleading.

I would argue, therefore, that the contempt for television and the emphasis on the auteur are the two dominant problems for European cinema and that they amount to the same thing: a determination to ignore audiences. It could be argued that the conclusion to this would be the abandonment of all subsidy for film production – surely if the audience is what counts there is no need to provide any subsidy at all. Existing audiences will simply determine the profitability, or not, of any form of production. My point, however, is not to homogenise audiences. What is important is to understand how a subsidy could work in relation to an audience, and that European film must look to producers who will in turn look for the majority of their funding from public service television. On this point, as on so much else, the British government has failed both its own national constituency and its European partners throughout the 80s and into the 90s. It has failed to notice the virtues of its own accidentally created subsidy system, nor promoted a discussion of the complexity of the relation between subsidy and audience. Instead, it has allowed Channel 4 to begin a remorseless drift out of public service: the subsidy system that it created by accident is now being destroyed with equal lack of care.

Notes

1. This often depends on the specific reasons as to why the board was set up in the first place. Interests represented can include such diverse factors as facility houses, producers, directors, unions and cultural interests.
2. See Ben Gibson, 'Seven Deadly Myths'.
3. I would not wish to deny that there are exceptions. Unfortunately (or

27

perhaps fortunately), I have never seen a Bresson movie on television, but he is one film-maker who I would doubt would make the transition. It is not simply that he is relatively unconcerned with spectacle or narration but, more unusually, he is not even concerned with the beauty of any individual image. His films are constructed by an extraordinary articulation of images, and the remorseless logic of his films may only function when the image is of a size sufficient to ensure its domination of the audience's attention.

SEVEN DEADLY MYTHS
Film Policy and the BFI, a Personal Lexicon

Ben Gibson

Since the 1950s the BFI has been involved, via the Experimental Film Fund and then the BFI Production Board, in low-budget film production. Recently it has become directly engaged in political advocacy, helping to provide a forum for debate on the future of British film production as a whole. I believe this new function is a vital one to which the Institute can make an important contribution. If the BFI is to continue to develop this role, however, its policies must be informed by a rigorous reading of its own history, in terms of a critical assessment of its own efforts in film production, as well as the histories and assumptions of other 'influential players'.

I am not concerned here with whether the participants in the Downing Street Seminar had either realistic expectations or informed tactical readings of the government's thinking on the film industry. Some items on the agenda have been taken up, others not. I am keen to identify the British film industry's attempts to find common causes, priorities and ambitions, and to examine how carefully such questions have been thought through. This enquiry leads me to lay out a lexicon of key assumptions, some of which have clouded the central issues debated at the infamous meeting on 16 June 1990 at Downing Street between Mrs Thatcher and the film industry. Of necessity it asks more questions than it attempts to answer. Moreover, it is unashamedly based on a partisan reading of current British cinema – from the point of view of BFI Production and its constituency. Where necessary I have indicated these partial views and their provenance.

The British Film Industry
While under this item I would also wish to interrogate the casual use (and abuse) of the terms 'commercial' and 'mainstream', I feel that the concept 'industry' is the most effective lever into the discussion, so I have left the others for discussion later.

Feature films are, of course, produced and distributed in this country, but I would contend that when we talk about the 'British film

29

industry' what is actually being described is a small service sector of the British television industry which also sells to a globalised theatrical distribution industry as a secondary form of recoupment/potential profit. The American film industry and the British television industry, by way of contrast, qualify as 'true' industries: they have producers, wholesalers and retailers, are dependent on enough consumers to sustain a chain of capital and have an infrastructure which implies 'demand'. (Taking the automobile industry as a metaphorical comparison, what we are talking about is the production of whole cars and established dealerships, rather than the provision of the occasional containerful of radiators or headlights.) Consequently, the British film industry has neither an element of strategic business planning adequate to its capital risk, nor does it have the R. & D. or 'product development' capacities to allow it to innovate, except through the occasional accident.

Just as critics have been in the habit, since Grierson published *World Film News* in the 30s, of reviewing British films as policy briefs for a national cinema rather than as part of any wider debates, so too are British producers endlessly embroiled in the process of attempting to establish an industry to be a part of. The anecdotal history tells us, of course, that seeing yourself as the centre (Alexander Korda, Rank, Lew Grade and Goldcrest) of something does not exactly encourage self-reflection or innovation, which more often than not tends to occur at the iconoclastic margins (Michael Balcon, Powell and Pressburger, Free Cinema, *Film on Four* and the BFI Production Board). But in doing so, they also perpetuated an idea now in its death throes: that there were the resources to justify a viable centre of a British film industry in the first place.

In autumn 1991, at a London seminar for film producers from Eastern European countries trying to come to terms with a new 'market', I felt it very necessary to point out that there were at present only two cinema-based film production industries in the world which sustained a consistent capital flow without state intervention: in the USA and India. An obvious point, but one which British producers' pride often serves to repress.

There can be no clearer indication that the industry is without a sense of a viable centre than the inclusion of the British Film Institute (a grown-up consumers' organisation, hardly equivalent to the MPAA or the Royal Television Society) high on the roster of relevant organisations to debate film policy. While in my opinion this is a positive development, what the BFI must help to do is see what factors, other than its own diligent efforts, led to it occupying such an important position. In particular, it must acknowledge this crucial lack of a centre.

30

Then there are cultural choices to consider. The BFI's formulation *Moving Image Culture* is definitely a cultural category, as opposed to an economic category, and its use tends to cover up the infrastructural disabilities of cinema. However, the best way of involving government (and their tax authorities in particular) in the invention of a film industry is to marshall our arguments in relation to *both* a set of cultural priorities and the much vaunted 'economic realities' which became the rhetoric of the 80s. The cultural priorities, I would argue, need to address the following questions:

- which market do we want to serve?
- does a 'national cinema' have a national cultural significance, or should it?
- does it matter who makes British films?
- can we see formation as distinct from the processes of production?
- given that television drama is quite viable, what are our arguments for making films?

I shall explore some of these questions below.

Europe = Subsidy

The current debate runs thus: Europe provides subsidy to promote a variety of cultural activities including film-making. It is held to be very damaging to the British film industry not to have any subsidy, yet on the other hand we suspect that subsidy would lead to a dependent low-budget industry without an audience (on the current German model). Consequently, it is considered inappropriate, so there is no political will to lobby for it. While there is some sense in part of this argument – I am not claiming that subsidy *per se* is a good idea, but neither are many professionals in the heavily-subsidised European industries – there are many other issues to be considered.

For instance, the British do have a tendency to start from the point that culture and commerce necessarily work in opposite directions. Consequently, cultural subsidy equals gravy, which makes for un-popular films. This may be so in some cases, but what is crucial is the acknowledgement that the MEDIA 95 programme is an industrial development programme, not a slush fund. It might run at a deficit, but then again so does British Screen, which has the same basic fiscal aim. Moreover, despite its cultural priorities, BFI Production is in the business of making investments in projects and not simply providing grants.

Returning to the precarious state of the 'industry' outlined above, from the point of view of BFI Production, the fewer feature-film 'starts' there are per year, and the deeper the perceived crisis, the more our marginality seems an affectation, even at an economic level. Over five years, for instance, a £1 million Terence Davies feature seems to have an equal chance of viability as a low-budget thriller featuring a pop star. Which begs the question: who is involved in commerce and who is producing culture?

The problem is that British producers, partly because so few are involved in a wide range of distribution, have very little real information or experience with regard to specialist markets for cinema films. If they do not believe there can be a market for a more 'European' kind of film, they are hardly likely to work towards the creation and development of one. Yet, given that we associate Europe with a cultural imperative, the cultivation of such a market (or markets) presents the possibility of integrating culture and commerce. The economic bottom line in terms of the relationship between a film's costs and its potential market-place remains, but the concept of the market-place (and the tastes of audiences with it) becomes much more sophisticated, with the possibility of greater specialisation. This effectively counteracts the notion that commercial viability is bound up with middlebrow, mid-Atlantic, populist entertainment.

However, when considered in relation to its major continental counterparts, it is hard to reject the old argument that what British cinema really needs to exist, let alone to be in a position to develop markets, is an adequate industrial infrastructure. That calls for more than tax concessions – it requires significant strategic investment.

Amphibious Cinema can always be Cinema
The argument goes: a film is designated thus simply by getting theatrical distribution, in any way, for whatever amount of time. It is therefore unnecessary to define a film in any legal sense. Whatever else it might have achieved, the removal of the Eady levy ended the automatic registration of films by the DTI. There are two major reasons why we spend so much time arguing about the aesthetic differences between cinema films and television films. On the one hand, it is an interesting and complicated aesthetic argument, particularly in a country where TV drama is arguably one of our most significant and pioneering forms of cultural production. On the other hand, it is precisely because we lack any agreed mechanism (outside trade union agreements) for distinguishing between cinema films and films made for television.

The question of the relationship between cinema and television in Britain is nevertheless a central one, transcending mere aesthetics, as I pointed out at the beginning of this paper. In other European countries television companies are heavily involved with cinema, but not as the principal producer and financier (and by implication, domestic exhibitor) as is the case in Britain. This has made the film/television definition less problematic. For example, in France the *Avance sur recettes* scheme relates to a law which says that something legally defined as a film shall not be broadcast on television until at least eighteen months after its date of completion.

Even then, however, European TV companies still invest much more money in cinema than do their British counterparts. To take the most extreme contrast available: the French television industry currently spends, according to the Centre National du Cinéma, around £110 million per year on French cinema. In the UK it is estimated that the production value of the BBC films which get (almost accidentally) theatrical exposure is around £3 million, while Channel 4 spends £12 million on *Film on Four*. There are no figures for Channel 3 stations, but it would be surprising if the total spent on domestic cinema in Britain was one fifth of the French figure.

A regular complaint is that whereas in many European countries TV stations will pay up to 35 per cent of a film's total budget for just one transmission, the situation in the UK is that a TV company will get a number of transmissions, for a specified period of years, against its investment. But we should remember that the British cinema cannot complain about the prices for which it *voluntarily* presells films to TV. Obviously, it would be desirable for the British television industry to make major subventions into the film production industry, as they are obliged to do by law in many other European countries such as Germany, France and Spain. But then British film-making is not seen as a highbrow-enough activity deserving of subsidy by TV executives. Many of their programmes are much more minority-oriented than the films. So how do we untangle this partnership and what are the reasons for doing so?

There seems to be a cycle of effects which determines the kind of low-budget cinema we get (and therefore what kind of mid- and high-budget film-makers we have produced) based on this TV relationship. A *Film On Four* on completion will be shown to UK film distributors. Some are taken on for exhibition, some not. It is rare that such films take enough money at the box office to pay back their promotional costs. In the case of a foreign film, that distributor would be setting such a (marginal) loss against the percentage of local television rights awarded to them by the film's producer. Thus the system makes sense of it all, allowing another film to be bought by the distributor and so on.

However, in the case of British films where the TV licensor is also the producer/financier, a different system operates. The television company wants the revenues from the cinema release and the general visibility that theatrical distribution can provide, usually about one year before the film is transmitted, in order to boost prestige and (hopefully) the subsequent television audience. But as producers they take no risk position in the theatrical viability of their films. Their own investment will be represented as rights plus equity, the equity recoupable against all kinds of rights exploitation in various markets. Thus, in their own minds, they have not made a theatrical film. They have, in business terms, made a TV film with additional theatrical spin-off possibilities.

I should like to suggest an alternative state of affairs by starting with the question of what is and what is not a film. This can only be defined in terms of length of theatrical hold-off against TV, and by law. But, it could be argued, if such a definition were to operate, television producers would merely opt more exclusively to make TV films. To this there are two responses. First, an aesthetic one: if we try to develop the formal integrity of our television in terms of the potential one medium can offer, we shall probably make better work. To my mind, this is what the 'quality television' argument is all about, with the obvious proviso that most films work quite well on television while most TV does not work in the cinema. Second, the vineyard system (making films this year for transmission one or two years after completion) which has allowed Channel 4 to sustain the industry we still have almost single handedly, is not about budgets but about cultural intentions. If we free ourselves from the idea that film must cost more than television drama, then this system should be attractive to British television producers if they can wait two years before transmission.

The radical proposal would be to cash flow two years of BBC production against self-imposed quotas of cinema films rather than television films. Of course, the commissioning executives need a way to swap these around in status, since definitions are problematic, as I have indicated. But the fact that 'TV films' often use energy rather than production values to storm the world specialist theatrical markets ought to have some implications for TV production policy. For BFI Production, making no more than three features a year, it is painful to see the film-making talent around the UK making its compromises with television audiences and swallowing its cinema ambitions. In places with different cultural priorities and industrial power bases, like Toronto, New York and Sydney, low- and mid-budget film-makers make London look like a backwater of specialist English-language film-making.

What if the BBC does not want the subvention? Of course they should have the right to produce work for their own audiences, but

34

perhaps they should be taxed and the revenue given to film production, as in so many other countries.

We Do Not Really Need a Home Audience
if We Can Get a Foreign One

Not many producers would express it in this way – of course they want as big an audience as they can get, especially at home. But the basis of the handful of really strong home markets in Europe (France with around 35 per cent and Italy with around 18 per cent) are laws which make it necessary to exploit home product over a given period theatrically. I would argue that we cannot have a film culture unless we get a home audience, and without a film culture we cannot make better films.

There are numerous questions to be dealt with here: the shortage of cinemas; the amount of coverage and promotion given to UK films in our print media; the problems I have described for the distributors; offshore cinema ownership; whether the cinema provokes cultural debate; which kind of market we address. For the BBC it is very common that a British film is available for theatrical release in all territories but the country of production.

What kind of films should we produce? I am persuaded that a home audience would initially be built on films which provoke national debates about cultural identity, the present and the future, in any genre. At twenty-six films last year, there simply is not enough cinema to generate such debate. Producers and film-makers would have to examine the specialist market-place and work in relation to its international rules and trends. The reality is that we have a cinema based on old paperback novels somebody liked, and television which is often, and popularly, about our everyday lives. The question, therefore, is how to displace the 'cutting edge' in the direction of cinema.

Yet are British producers prepared to go along with this? It is hard to think of another national film industry which has for so long, in so many guises, tried to second-guess foreign consumers and produce for export. But there is no doubt that the limited success of the kind of film associated with the Curzon, Mayfair, and the films of Merchant/Ivory, disguises a deeper failure to keep pace with the concerns of a local audience.

What of the challenging and exciting films that are occasionally made and which deserve wider distribution? Outside the realm of production, the BFI must concern itself with the home distribution of low-budget British material. I think it should take the radical step of encouraging regional film theatres to continue to run films which are doing good business but scheduled to close. This might reveal an

35

actual shortage of screens, which is being hidden by short runs and monthly repertory programming.

Leave Formation to Film Schools

On one level, of course, they can do it – that is what they are for. But the film and television industries are apprentice-based talent pools. If the film-making infrastructure has holes, most of them reflect a failure to deal with the heterogeneity of our possible future film industry, and its fostering.

The policy of the National Film and Television School, our best-funded school, in these bad times seems to be graduating people to work in Los Angeles, at the BBC, or in advertising. Given the economic climate, this is fair enough on one level since the business of a school is to train people for work. But this priority, carried out too rigidly, can create a terrible shortage of 'further experiences' for the potentially successful nonconformists. Perhaps it is a matter of recruiting more defiant students, and of realising that part of the audience at a graduation show is hungry for eccentricity, and for rough edges.

At the other end of the scale we have art schools, which are under-funded, where a lot of people are permitted or encouraged to ignore narrativity and 'mainstream' film-making altogether. What we do not have at present is a middle ground, a place where the creative low-budget film-makers of tomorrow can learn their craft. There are not, of course, enough BFI movies made each year for it to justify too much attention from educationalists. The point is not to pander to an imaginary mainstream or refuse it without first of all defining it.

BFI Production is involved, as it always has been, at the level of providing an outlet for some kinds of risk and experiment, both in shorts and features, and, like everyone involved in film production, it is also involved in information. In terms of the employability of British film-makers, the accidental transformation of a made-for-TV film into a small-scale theatrical release can make a career. However, if we are to deal with new markets more actively, in particular with European cinema audiences, we cannot assume we have an appropriate training base for such an ambition, or that we produce enough 'beginners' slope' films. France last year made as many first features as our total output.

This is one of the places in the debate where the role of the BFI seems to bear a specially strong relation to the economic future of the film production industry. The Lloyd Report in the late 60s and the setting up of the NFTS has had important results, and the BFI might now play the role of asking what our training needs are for the 90s. I suspect that the 'industry' communicates its needs to the education system either inefficiently or not at all, and that its own educational responsibilities, like training in ITV, have been 'put on the back burner' alongside the creation of Jobfit.

Studios Are Good ... for Big Films

At BFI Production two of the strongest debates about the strategy for the next five years are: (1) Can you make good work without specialist production environments (namely studios)? and (2) Whatever happened to low-budget cinema films? The questions are interrelated, of course. One of the reasons the BFI operates as a kind of hybrid financier/producer is to provide a space to develop some accumulation of low-budget expertise and some economies of scale.

It is important that at this stage the recent history of British feature production be examined from the point of view of production environments, their ethos, their economies of scale and, above all, the thoroughness of the way in which larger production environments (studio production) cover stages of preparation for film-making and evolve methods of decision-making based on films, not deals.

The BBC, with its studio system, produced much of Britain's interesting work in modestly-budgeted single dramas, but cinema film producers have no equivalent base. It might be that a loosely-structured studio environment, based around a block of small producers' offices, is an infrastructural necessity, or that those who finance feature production should concentrate on building strong, enduring and flexible production houses from those that already exist. This base cannot come into existence without better producers' shares of returns on the work, and a more generous approach to copyright and sales arrangements from the financiers.

A High Low Budget is a Good Low Budget, and a Big One is Better

Finally, a question which follows on from the previous one. Why is Britain one of the most expensive places in the world to make a low-budget film? We spend time on deals which we lose on preparing films; we have a Hollywood-based production system; our training system is not based sufficiently on creative solutions to poverty.

Many of the film industry representatives who took part in the Downing Street Seminar subscribe to the argument that all films made for less than £2.5 million (the figure may have gone up) come in the category of pure culture because they cannot recoup their costs, let alone generate a profit for commercial investors. There simply is not enough 'above the line' (star casting, and so on) to make them marketable, or so the argument goes; thus some of them seek financial assistance from government to make films of a mid- to high-budget scale. If we suppose that the government might legitimately ask them to be self-supporting, with a few small tax concessions to be in this kind of business, should not an organisation like the BFI also be researching the validity of their claim?

I have not done the research myself, and I know there is a declining market for what used to be called 'B' movies (and are now called 'video titles'). But in a highly fragmented world media industry, low-budget films like *Drugstore Cowboy* and *Sex, Lies and Videotape* can and do compete. So do British productions like *My Beautiful Laundrette, Letter to Brezhnev* and *Truly, Madly, Deeply*. More and more the low-budget genres are coming together into an informed, cine-literate market-place, based largely on authors' reputations. It is also harder and harder to define an individual work within the range from Exploitation/Schlock to High Art to Punk/Sleaze, but that does not make it impossible to sell the films.

So why make lower-budget films? We all want our money to go further, of course. At present, in a year which saw a mere twenty-six British films, every provocative, ambitious first feature has a lot of baggage to carry; it is either a watershed or a waste of money. There simply are not enough films or a sufficiently well-established theatrical audience to make more of a debate than that. At BFI Production we are currently talking about films that cost around £500,000 (a *Film on Four* these days costs around £800,000 to £1,300,000).

Low budgets create a wider access to film production; they provide a lower-risk financing structure in which a smaller range of people want to be pleased all of the time; they create a space where the film-makers of the future can develop their craft instead of the crafts of partying and deal-making in the years of preparation for each project.

It should be remembered that Britain is the country that bought us the 'quota quickie', that unique film school of the 30s, with graduates of the calibre of Michael Powell and Alfred Hitchcock. They had some simple rules: over sixty minutes and under seventy-five; use stock footage wherever possible; tell a story and come in at £1 a foot. I am not suggesting a return to such a system, obviously, but we must recognise that film-makers need the opportunity to practise and develop their craft in a cost-effective manner.

Conclusion

At a Labour Party seminar on film policy (held in the National Film Theatre on 18 September 1991), Mark Fisher MP appealed to the film community to 'speak with one voice'. There is no doubt that we are all in the same industry, trying to increase and make more consistent our productive capacity. What is not so easy is agreeing which strategies are strategies and which are rhetoric and received ideas posing as analysis. By examining some of the dominating orthodoxies of the debate, we might just be able to fight for a common cause, rather than

38

assume its existence for a day at a time when it suits us. Rather than simply provide a secretariat for a wide range of vested interests in the area of film policy, the BFI must engage with the complexity of such a great task – to have a 'British film industry' worthy of its own boasts.

CHANGING CONDITIONS OF INDEPENDENT PRODUCTION IN THE UK

Richard Paterson

The increasing role of independent production in the changing environment of British television was the result of one of the most successful lobbying campaigns of the 80s. It was a period when the existing boundaries between firms within the TV industry were shifting in response to competitive, technological and regulatory changes. The legitimate efforts of self-interested groups using a particular ideology, related to a very different policy for the organisation of the television industry, placed the *status quo* under severe strain.

The conditions for 'independent' production in the film and television industry in Britain are explored and analysed in this paper.[1] The emphasis is on the realm of the contractual, resonating with the everyday concerns within the independent sector. Much work remains to be done on non-market governance forms in the firm, although there has been an increasing literature on the area of transaction-cost economics in recent years.[2] The value of this analysis is that it brings together the discourse of the legal and the economic into the domain of the sociological, in terms of operational effectiveness of a particular industry.

The UK television industry offers a case study of an evolving series of contractual relationships affected by commercial and industrial policy. Conditions for creativity have taken second place to a market orientation in TV production which, it could be argued, has undermined the vitality of the sector. This restructuring has highlighted the efficient boundaries of the firm. The imposition of different governance structures is a key factor in the redefinition of the British audiovisual space predicated on the desire to lower the barriers to entry. In the British film industry, different structures have been created in the separate context of 'international' film production.[3]

Any account of 'independent' production must define the factors of dependency and mutuality in any relationship between contracting parties, including any regulatory dimensions. Here I want to suggest that vertical integration may not be a necessary condition of effective, efficient programme production, although it has only proved to be possible to otherwise organise production where the domestic market is of a much larger size than in Britain. A changing set of firms in the audiovisual sector may have created the possibility of new governance structures. One major problem for Britain's industry is that, though regulatory changes were necessary, for a variety of reasons, those imposed put the wrong emphasis on one preferred firm type (the small independent producer) at a crucial juncture in the development of the industry. The dogma of competition between small firms misrecognised the need for efficient boundaries between firms. The disavantages of the disaggregated structure are considerable for audiovisual production industries with small domestic markets.

In essence, one part of my argument is that the medium-sized production and distribution enterprises that emerged in the UK commercial television sector after 1955 will be lost through the imposition of a different mode of governance in commercial television, particularly after 1993, to the detriment of the moving image industry in Britain. The medium-sized TV enterprise should have been of particular significance at this juncture of international (and particularly European) expansionism with strong cross-border growth. It is interesting to note that Canal Plus's original investment in TVS was based on a perception that they could benefit from UK television's long commercial experience.

Assured distribution and secure funding remains a central factor for any financially viable cultural production, and is related to the functions carried out by a firm and its optimum size. This is one of the reasons (although arguably not the most important) why the BBC should retain its critical mass, integrated structure and central role (at least for now) in British cultural production as it evolves in the new European structures post-1992. It is imperative that the BBC's introduction of an internal market within its own operations following the introduction of 'Producer's Choice' does not undermine this capability.

Governance Structures
In any firm with a strategic core and sufficient critical mass, transactions are internalised with a vertically integrated structure to retain and maximise the use of those core skills. Other parts of the production process will be externalised in contractual relationships. The nature of such contracts must be viewed as a key element in a framework for creativity inasmuch as they affect performance patterns. Furthermore, they are bound up with the definition of the efficient boundary of the firm. There is a fundamental difference, semantic and real, between independence secured from secure funding and dependence on commissioning editors or banks or whoever. Firm size,

41

degree of integration, and financial resources underpin a series of relationships which affect the creative process.

Transactions in the context of TV production are determined by questions of specificity, uncertainty and frequency. There are three possible outcomes: market governance, bilateral governance (relational) or unified governance (vertical integration). The results of recent attempts in television to move to bilateral or market governance indicate the specificity of cultural production and the difficulty and unsuitability of imposed market governance forms to an industry of insufficient size. Efficient boundaries between firms have been unsettled by recent changes, both those intrinsic to the system (technical change) and those externally imposed (reregulation). There is further cause for concern that the core skills base of the industry might be dissipated as a result of changes with deleterious cultural effects.

In the film and television production sectors in the United States analysts found that 'fixed costs associated with lumpy, indivisible inputs (such as sound stages) need not be covered by the individual firm'.[4] In the USA the smooth functioning of a rental market makes it possible for the industry to exploit economies of scale. But the same authors also commented that 'in an unstable rental market it may pay a firm to own its inputs as a precaution against fluctuations in the rental price'. The UK has all the hallmarks of instability and, in film, with its international orientation, dependency. Regulation is one means used to forestall or remedy these problems in other countries.

Boundaries between firms change as an industry matures or its modes of operation change. Unsurprisingly, there has been a dynamism in a number of sectors in the UK film and television industry in the light of the perception of the possibility of serving a multiplication of audiovisual production entities in the burgeoning corporate video, satellite and advertising industries. The facilities sector grew on the calculation that it could operate effectively and profitably in a growing market-place, a miscalculation by several firms of the maturity of the market which has led to a series of closures and large redundancies.[5]

One interesting, and little-commented change, which went against the trend of disaggregation was the decision by Channel 4 to house its own advertising sales department. This was the more curious in the circumstances of the ITV companies employing separate companies to sell their advertising and the Channel's own history of maintaining the bare minimum of headquarters staff.

The current transitional period in the industry is undoubtedly the reason for uncertainties, which have been exacerbated by the high risk which the regulatory and business changes have brought in their wake. For example, the demise of BSB had a major effect at many levels of the TV programme production industry. There has been a view that new principles of production and business organisation are emerging in Western industrialised societies which would be confirmed by an examination of TV production companies in the 80s (although this might well turn out to be a temporary aberration).[6] Asset specificity is a means of reducing risk for larger companies in certain industrial settings. Variable contractual relationships can act as a way of absorbing cycles of change within sectors, although the larger companies are better able to withstand the troughs and to benefit at the expense of smaller companies.

The large or medium-size television organisations in which transfer and interaction took place internally had positive features, testified to by the productivity in creative terms of these enterprises. Their functions have become increasingly fragmented. As Oliver Williamson notes, 'efficiency purposes are served by matching governance structures to the attributes of transactions in a discriminating way' and, as I have argued elsewhere, such was the beneficent relationship which underpinned the old order in Britain's TV industry.[7]

Television

The early days of commercial television witnessed the emergence of a few independent production companies[8] but these were effectively shut out as the system developed. 'Independents' returned to the stage in TV production in the early 80s, a variegated group of companies enticed by the founding of Channel 4. With the growth in output and the, for some, surprising ability of 'independents' to provide programming, the numbers grew to over 500 in 1989–90, supplying some 2140 hours of Channel 4's output.[9] In 1981 the Independent Programme Producers' Association was formed to represent the interests of the 250 companies working for Channel 4. Alongside this, the BFTPA were treating with the ITV companies and the film majors on a series of parallel issues mainly concerning industrial relations matters. This was a long-standing relationship often involving wholly owned subsidiaries of the ITV companies, although not without its own contradictions. The television agreement (the ITCA agreement) was used in parallel with the BFPA/BFTPA agreement for crewing TV productions and led to internal union disputes as the gradual demise of Britain's film industry put ever more stress on TV production.[10] In the new circumstances of Channel 4 and the removal of many of the barriers to entry (indeed, there was a positive encouragement to enter the market) a new set of boundaries between firms were devised and new agreements negotiated (the Terms of Trade).

The Channel 4 policy was to create a number of companies, 'poor but stable',[11] with a restricted ability to grow. The Channel determined early in its existence that it would not be reliant on a few major suppliers which might begin to act in concert against Channel 4's best economic interests. In this situation perhaps eight companies a year received deals in excess of £1 million. Channel 4 acted as the business school for the independents, imposing effective cost control and cost reporting based on very detailed budgets and schedules, and with a cost-plus system introduced via the Terms of Trade. It established a contractual norm with suppliers adapted subsequently by the BBC. The Channel was effectively the independents' banker and provider of cash flows with programme price based on a cost-plus basis with a production fee (profit margin) added on. The programme's value in the schedule was not assessed and the Channel retained rights in the programmes it had financed, with net profits on further sales split 70/30 in the Channel's favour.

There is now some unhappiness at this contractual system, and a debate, and lobbying of government, has been joined concerning ownership of rights, particularly in a changing media economy where programme library sales to secondary markets are seen to be of increasing importance. The independents view the current situation as a financial strait-jacket but, of course, unless they bring money to the table they have no power.

Unsurprisingly, in the light of the transaction-economics model, the independent producers see much of the desirability of becoming integrated companies, producing and selling, in revising the boundaries of their operations. They maintain the ideological stance against the broadcasters whom they now try to imitate (this, of course, was highlighted even more strongly in the participation of 'independents' in Channel 3 franchise bids either as part-shareholders or through tied output deals).

Trade Associations
IPPA has been described by some as the most successful lobbying operation of the 80s. The role of the trade association has been defined as: responding to intra-industry competition, reacting to the market power or organisational efforts of the industry's transaction partner, and responding to state regulation of the industry.[12] The reactive nature of these roles is normative, but in the case of the independent producers' lobby they were matched by the attempt to set the agenda and further to revise the contractual and transactional relationship. It was a political as well as an economic/trade lobby. IPPA's role has been of considerable economic (and ideological) interest and importance in the changing place of the independent producer.

There is, of course, a great potential for internal conflicts within any trade association, despite any restrictions on membership. These pos-

44

sibilities have now increased in the merger of IPPA and the Producers' Association as PACT, with the possibility of divisions between larger companies interested in different contractual arrangements and those many small companies working happily within the Terms of Trade. In comparison the ITVA (itself the site of internal struggles over a number of years[13]) had less cause for disunity, or perhaps a greater cause for presenting a united front, but failed to carry its arguments to government and maintain the specificities of its own very specific contractual arrangements. The ITVA's diversion to wider business interests such as the Superchannel venture, when every ITV company (except Thames) created a strategic alliance to enter the European market, and which failed badly, might be seen to have been one cause, among many others, for its ineffectual lobbying on its own behalf.

IPPA, on the other hand, was in a sense pushing at an open door. A government discenchanted with first the BBC, and then later the high revenues and politically indiscreet practices of the ITV companies, was only too happy to support the entrepreneurial remit which 'independents' seemed to offer. It fitted perfectly with the received wisdoms of early Thatcherism. The independents claimed to be purposive, innovative and different, but have ended up locked in battle over the 'publishing' contractual relationship. It is this publishing relationship between programme supplier and broadcaster/distributor which the Annan Report had suggested as a means of breaking the power of the duopoly but which has been the stalking horse for the disintegrating tendencies which so mark the reregulated television industry.

The Peacock Report on the future financing of the BBC further unsettled the received ideologies in British broadcasting by recommending a quota of 40 per cent independent production on all channels. Its arguments were based on a series of incorrect analogies of TV production to magazine publishing. They constituted an attempt to regulate a market in domestic programme-making into existence.[14] The independents' 25 Per Cent Campaign was quickly followed by the action of the Home Office to implement a 25 per cent quota of independent productions on both the BBC and ITV Channel 3 in the Broadcasting Act of 1990. These impositions were the outcome of systematic lobbying against the ITV cartel and the BBC, but were underpinned more by political ideology than analysis of possible effects on the industry.

The Firm Types

Television production by independent producers underwent considerable change through the 80s. The needs and roles of these companies can be analysed using three ideal types.[15] It is particularly apposite to my argument to note how the differential contracting arrangements determine different independent firm types.

1. On the first tier are small companies with a turnover of less than £500,000 per annum. These companies may be seen as enhanced freelances (or dependent casuals, depending on your viewpoint), and exist from the occasional commission using the home as the office and filling in with other work in down periods. The argument has been made that the most effective companies at this level act as niche players, with the proper financial controls necessary to run a small business. In the niche they act as a pole of attraction for specialist researchers, but have a need to maintain continuing direct access to commissioning editors (they are very expensive in terms of transaction costs). They also act as the most flexible variable for fluctuations in the market and bear the cost of downturn more heavily than the larger companies. Their marginal viability is particularly exacerbated by the tendency of these companies to specialise in the shrinking market for factual programming. Experiments by Channel 4 in subcommissioning proved less than creatively or contractually successful in sustaining these small companies.

2. At the second tier are the thirty or so companies with a turnover of up to £2 million. These are run as proper businesses and are aggressive players in seeking commissions. After differing lengths of operation these companies have made the move beyond the hand-to-mouth existence in constant supplication to Channel 4 into more usual business practices including the search for equity investment, the securing of co-financing packages. They tend to oppose the Terms of Trade which allowed their establishment, and wish to seek a return on the 'value' of the programme in the schedule rather than on a cost-plus basis. It is these companies, too, which have found it easiest to expand beyond the traditional Channel 4 supplier role. The directions of development have been towards the secure series commission (sometimes tied to a form of output deal), with the clear intent of reducing financial vulnerability by extending activity. It is also clear to these companies that development is a priority, and having been bankrolled by the cost-plus system of payment pioneered by Channel 4 they now seek to erect barriers to entry by other companies by using a market-dominant position to control key commissions. It is these companies, too, which are most at risk in the new conditions of the market, with the undercapitalised, in particular, likely to be merged or taken over by other companies.

Some of these companies are now creating a firm profile which is similar to the smaller ITV companies, with increased output and visibility across all channels. This is a case of transactional trust ('you know who you're dealing with') replacing the commission-led contract, a version of in-house production without the transactional economies of integrated operations. Such companies seeking to create efficient boundaries between themselves and suppliers or commissioners have also diversified into other areas of activity including facilities, studios and corporate video production so that, for instance, Mentorn now draws 30 per cent of its income from renting out video facilities. One way of looking at this situation is to see it as the reinvention of the ITV system in a new structure, but without the important access to income at the point of distribution (namely, broadcasting).

3. The third tier of companies are the large, fully capitalised companies such as Carlton/Zenith (now set to change places with disenfranchised Thames Television) and Crown Communications with diversified media interests including the ownership of or shareholding in facilities and commercial radio or television franchises. These companies differ little from the five major ITV companies other than the absence of the right to broadcast terrestrially.

The key analytical factors which these developments signal concern the structures of organisations and their mode of governance. These are factored by a changing series of contractual relationships, and different boundaries between firms, in the evolving audiovisual production sector. The modes of analysis required are sociological in terms of motivations, legal in terms of regulatory and contractual requirements, and economic in terms of the efficiencies and inefficiencies of the transactional dimension.

Film

The parlous state of film production in Britain and the legislative neglect which has allowed this to occur underlines the significance of the recent debates about television. The importance of the secure funding of production companies able to develop a serious international marketing capability with a portfolio of films has stumbled in the UK against the whims of investors, the lack of a studio structure, the difficulties in securing rights, and so on.[16]

In the 80s, 454 'British' feature films were produced with the participation of no less than 342 companies. Film production in Britain has a peculiarly dependent structure of governance. The efficient boundary for the firm is defined in its international and dependent context and relates as often to an individual as to any strategic industrial concerns. At its simplest the lack of a studio structure inhibits investment, and the myths surrounding the failure of the proto-studio, Goldcrest, sustains the difficulties perceived by investors. The development of any one feature will have its costs written off against that particular investment rather than against other successful investments, because often the company is set up for the production of a single film. Presales in foreign markets take on an over-large importance.

Film's different modes of governance also, then, need to be reviewed within the framework of transaction-cost analysis and particularly an understanding of how the contractual relationships operate. The firm types are very varied but without the range in size of independent television production companies.

The Enigma/Puttnam arrangement is based on the reputation of one film-maker, David Puttnam, able to draw from a consortium of investing partners (a $55 million fund, drawing from Warner Bros $25 million, Fujisankei $10 million, County NatWest $10 million, and originally BSB $10 million). It was responsible for financing *Memphis Belle*.[17] Enigma concentrate on developing and producing films and do not get diverted into questions of corporate financing or broader corporate strategy.

Working Title (now wholly owned by Polygram, a major record company) is established under a record-label-type arrangement with companion operations. The virtue of this structure is that it allows the operation of a series of creative centres all of which receive administrative support from Polygram, while the production company concentrates on film and TV programme production. It is similar in philosophy to the 'housekeeping' deals struck by Hollywood majors, creating multiple independent film companies related to a studio. Working Title's distribution is through an independent film sales company, Manifesto, which is another subsidiary of Polygram.

A third firm type is personified by J & M Entertainment, which operates a system of contracts with producers but pays only on delivery of the finished product. It does not produce any films itself, but in conjunction with international partners can guarantee the budget on a film.

The crossover between film production and television production is exemplified through a number of firms which produce TV movies and mini-series for the international market, usually with co-financing partners, and with the budget usually 90 per cent covered before production starts. Such mixed production portfolios have become more prevalent in recent years.

For all film production companies, presales and video rights are highly determinate of what is produced. Margaret Matheson[18] noted several important factors in operating an independent film production company. The lack of development finance (the ability to write off monies on films not made) is the biggest problem for the independent UK film company, and any company serious about success needs to invest a minimum of £2 million to set up in business.

A key factor thereafter is the crucial arrangement of distribution by a distributor who both knows the market and has sufficient clout to sell programmes alongside other material in its portfolio. The decision of Zenith to take Paramount as a 49 per cent shareholder was based on its ability to enter the whole international market. It must be remembered that the US domestic market accounts for a large percentage of all theatrical film revenues. Audience reach becomes of principal importance in international film production compared with the primary domestic reach of most television to date. What we see, then, is a different governance structure dependent on international markets and international capital, a non-UK conditionality which determines the contractual interdependencies and efficient boundaries of these firms.

The absence of a studio system and the importance of distribution and presales have introduced a crucial intermediary in the structures which affect the independent film company's existence. This is the sales agent[19] who will package and develop material to secure finance. In this equation, budget, cast and crew need to be arranged to convince the financial partners and investors to put up their money. The sales company will seek both a primary sale to the domestic market (and primarily to a broadcaster) as well as presales to major territories, mainly through a minimum guarantee from a distributor. Without a vertically integrated industry the missing sectors need to be constituted to enable the efficient functioning of an 'industry'. These might emerge in the market or, as has been argued in the UK, need to be constituted through state aid or regulation.

Conclusions

So what conclusions can be drawn from the recent evolution and performance of the UK TV and film independents? Are the changing conditions marked by an internal dynamic, by external forces or by a combination of both? With what results for the moving image industry in terms of creativity and culture?

The analytical framework used here – of structures of governance, variable contracting and firm boundaries – underlines the role of industrial policy in defining firm types in the context of the markets for films or television programming. There are old arguments about British film – that it is alive and well and called television – but, more importantly in the changing political and economic framework of the 90s, we must look at changed audience targeting and the global framework within which audiences are in order to analyse the distinctions. Television has tended to speak to nation or region. It has had an assured, almost protected, market. Film has spoken across borders and 'internationally'. Perhaps now television's address is changing (MTV, CNN, Eurochannels), so that the domestic remit of television becomes increasingly untenable. Firms and organisations inhabit and react to the contexts within which they operate and these can be altered by a variety of factors.[20]

In a country like Britain there has been a regulatory framework for television which successfully engendered medium-sized national companies. Perhaps their time has passed or, because their managements failed to devise suitable policies for the new environment, they will be taken over. Companies need to reassess the 'international' opportunities seized so successfully by Canal Plus and by Silvio Berlusconi's companies. These are synergies which might be achieved through horizontal or vertical mergers both within national boundaries and in cross-border take-overs. Audiences need to be served in their multiple identities and with their diverse needs. Both national and European regulatory and governance structures should be ordered to achieve the desired ends if there is a desire to focus both an industry and a culture. The aftermath of the Downing Street Seminar seemed to learn from some of the mistakes of the broadcasting legislation in urging the need for the creation of an industrial structure.[21] With the debate about the renewal of the BBC charter about to commence, perhaps a radical review which does not ignore the conditions for creativity can take place and the role of the 'independent' can be looked at through a broader perspective than heretofore.

New associations and alliances can be created to achieve the desired objective which take account of these critical contractual and governance structures within which firms operate. As the changing conditions include an apparent tendency to oligopoly the regulatory change and optimum efficiency boundaries between firms need to be assessed. Priority should be given to an industrial policy which regulates for success rather than relying on a loose *laissez-faire* legal and economic framework. The cultural hazards attendant when a set of firms are subordinate to multinational companies needs to be foregrounded in any debate so that the public interest in securing adequate representations of its own heritage and cultural mores can be underpinned by suitable structures of governance.

Notes

1. This is a continuation of my analysis and argument in *Organising for Change* (London: BFI, 1990).
2. 'The basic notion of transaction-costs theory is that properties of the transaction determine what constitute the efficient governance structure ... institutional form and internal organisation matter when it comes to strategy', Torger Reve, 'The Firm as a Nexus of Internal and External Contracts', in Maschiko Aoki, Bo Gustafsson and Oliver E. Williamson,

50

The Firm as a Nexus of Treaties (London: Sage, 1990), p. 134. See also Oliver E. Williamson, *Economic Institutions of Capitalism* (New York: Free Press, 1985).

3. Nick Smedley and John Woodward, *Productive Relationships?* (London: BFI, 1991); Richard Lewis and Paul Marris, *Promoting the Industry* (London: BFI, 1991).

4. Bruce Owen, Jack H. Beebe and Willard G. Manning, *Television Economics* (Lexington, Mass: D.C. Heath, 1974).

5. Chris Dickinson, 'Downward spiral for facilities', *Broadcast*, 2 August 1991.

6. Michael H. Best, *The New Competition* (London: Routledge, 1990).

7. See Richard Paterson, 'The Economic Organisation of Television Production', in Richard Paterson (ed.), *Organising for Change* (London: BFI, 1990), and Oliver Williamson, *Economic Institutions of Capitalism*.

8. See John Woodward, 'Day of the Reptile: Independent Production Between the 80s and the 90s', in Richard Paterson (ed.), *Organising for Change*.

9. Jonathan Davies, *TV, UK – A special report* (London: Knowledge Research, in collaboration with IPPA and TPA, 1991).

10. Manuel Alvarado and John Stewart, *Made for Television: Euston Films* (London: BFI, 1985).

11. Woodward, op. cit.

12. See Aoki et al., op. cit.

13. See Bernard Sendall, *Independent Television in Britain*, vol. II, *Expansion and Change, 1958–68* (London: Macmillan, 1983).

14. See John Viera, 'Rerunning the Rhetoric: An Economic Analysis of the Effects of the Financial Interest and Syndication Rules from 1970 to 1991', Paper to 4th International Television Studies Conference, July 1991.

15. This model was first elucidated by John Woodward, op. cit., and used at the IPPA Seminar 'Do You Need to Change?: Surviving as a Producer in the 1990s', London, 4 December 1990.

16. See Richard Lewis, 'London's Importance as a Centre of International Film Sales', in Lewis and Marris, op. cit.

17. See 'Screen Finance focus on strategies for growth', *Screen Finance*, 18 October 1990.

18. Margaret Matheson at the Media Management Forum, University of Stirling, February 1990.

19. Richard Lewis, op. cit.

20. See Stig Hjarvard, 'Pan-European Television News: Towards a European Political Public Sphere?', Paper to 4th International Television Studies Conference, July 1991.

21. See Nick Smedley and John Woodward, *Productive Relationships?* (London: BFI, 1991).

LOW-BUDGET BRITISH PRODUCTION
A Producer's Account

James Mackay (with an introduction by Duncan Petrie)

Duncan Petrie

Anyone with even the remotest interest in the British film industry will know that it is in an almost permanent state of financial crisis. It is also an industry whose production sector is made up of a small number of production houses like Palace Productions, Handmade Films and Working Title (companies which often have a stake in other sectors of the industry, such as distribution), and a host of smaller companies often consisting of little more than an independent producer with a full-time assistant/secretary. The production slump currently affecting British cinema has made survival extremely difficult for the latter type of company. This state of affairs has essentially highlighted what is a structural problem within the industry. As Jane Headland and Simon Relph pointed out in a 1991 BFI publication which examines the current crisis: 'What is particular to Britain is a separation between exhibition, distribution and production which leaves the riskiest element of the process (the production sector) uniquely isolated and for which there is no fiscal or regulatory compensation.'[1]

The dissociation between distribution and production invariably favours the former sector at the expense of the latter. Even when British producers can get their films properly distributed, and the major distributors in this country favour the financial terms offered by Hollywood producers, they are the last to recoup any revenues. This leaves many small companies, who can often work on only one project at a time, surviving in a hand-to-mouth situation. Such a state of affairs has detrimental knock-on effects into other areas such as development and marketing. As Simon Perry, the new chief executive at British Screen puts it:

> Having recently been an independent producer myself, I know that too often you urgently need to get a film into production in order to pay the rent.
>
> That has two dire effects. One: not enough time is spent on

development, so a number of films have slouched into production with nobody quite sure whether the script was right, and two: the producer cannot buy himself enough time or is not sufficiently motivated to think about working on the film after it is finished.[2]

A further, but related, problem is linked to the ability of small production companies to recoup any monies over and above their production fee. Production companies will often invest a proportion of the budget of a project, along with other equity investors and distribution guarantees. The problem is that in the risky, rather cut-throat business of film finance every investor will want his money back as quickly as possible. Even a benevolent and adventurous (in terms of the projects they have been willing to back) investor like British Screen will insist on early – if not first – recoupment. What this does is make it increasingly difficult for small producers to make any money on projects, further exacerbating their financial vulnerability.

Yet small independent producers do manage to survive in the face of such adversity, driven along by a passionate belief in what they are doing. One of the most interesting examples in the British film industry is James Mackay, whose impressive list of credits include Derek Jarman's innovative feature films *The Last of England* and *The Garden*. This essay will examine Mackay's experiences of the British film industry in the 80s and into the 90s, a view from the margins (despite the cultural reputation and media exposure of Derek Jarman) which in some ways is a very typical story while in others is unique.

James Mackay

The area I have tended to work in is mainly low-budget films, some with narrative but largely music based – what I would term 'sound and image composite' films. They come in different shapes and sizes but one thing they all have in common, apart from one documentary that I have done, is that they are all aimed at the cinema and they are all primarily intended for cinema viewing. I am a fine art graduate of North East London Polytechnic, and I went there not because I wanted to pursue painting or sculpture but because I wanted to make films. I come from Inverness, and there was no other way in the mid-70s that I could see which gave me ready access to the tools of film-making. The National Film School which had just been founded and the London International Film School were largely postgraduate, and one you had to pay for and the other you had to have a degree to get into.

You cannot displace yourself from Inverness that easily and come to London and look for work in the film industry, so what I decided to do was to attach myself to a course of study which would give me access

53

to equipment. North East London Polytechnic advertised itself as having access to film-making equipment (thought this was not strictly true, as I later discovered), so I applied for a position there. The film-making I was interested in was largely European; I was influenced by people like Fellini, Godard, Welles, Warhol and Kenneth Anger so I thought art cinema was where I wanted to go. When I got to art college I met a group of film-makers and artists who were working in film and video and that certainly influenced the course that I took from then on. Whereas they were largely content with making work for a gallery situation, however, I always aimed towards the big screen, so I combined the two disciplines, fine art and film-making.

After leaving college I moved into exhibition, programming the cinema at the London Film Co-op for a couple of years in the late 70s and programming avant-garde films at the Edinburgh and Berlin Film Festivals. I met quite a few different film-makers at the Co-op and one evening Derek Jarman came along and showed some Super-8 films; it was through discussing the problems of working with Super-8 with him that I got involved with production and why a lot of the work I have subsequently done has been produced on Super-8.

Super-8 and Low-budget Production
The use of Super-8 in independent film-making, both in Britain and abroad, was a consequence of television news companies switching from 16-mm film to video for news reports. Many of the early film collectives used to receive free film stock and processing from the television companies and this facility disappeared when they moved to video. So you had the situation at the lower end of the film finance scale people who, had they been working in the late 60s and early 70s, would have worked on 16 mm, turning to Super-8 as a medium. Consequently, by the late 70s, the majority of the leading young and avant-garde film-makers in this country were working on Super-8.

I subsequently worked on a variety of Super-8 productions in the 80s, the majority with Derek Jarman, beginning with extremely modest short films. At the same time it did not seem feasible to instantly raise large amounts of money for a film project, whereas it seemed more realistic to go out and shoot something on Super-8, blow it up to 16 mm, and try to exhibit it in an art house cinema. The first film I produced, *TG Psychic Rally in Heaven*, an eight-minute short, cost something like £350. It was shot, processed, blown up to 16 mm and shown at the Berlin Film Festival within two weeks of its inception. We have susequently developed this approach to film-making in terms of vision, ambition, confidence and budgets, leading up to the production of *The Last of England* in 1987, a highly sophisticated and innovative feature film generated almost entirely on Super-8. This

54

demonstrates quite powerfully that with very small resources (in fact, *The Last of England* cost less than a quarter of a million pounds to make and it is a 35-mm Dolby stereo film) you can make quite a big impact.

In other words, you do not need to have vast amounts of money to make independent art films. This approach to film-making is a direct result of my experiences from learning my craft in a low-budget art school environment where you have £40 per term to pay for the materials to make films, to working at the London Film Co-op and at Berlin and Edinburgh, where I met many film-makers from around the world who also worked on small budgets and were involved in various alternative kinds of film-making. These experiences inspired me to strive to realise these 35-mm cinematic ambitions without the possibility of budgets that would just enable me to go out and shoot something on 35 mm and make films the normal way. The result was that the first films I did were very simple.

The Early Films
One of the early films I made was *What Can I Do With a Male Nude?* with director Ron Peck. This production was literally a 'home movie' in that it was shot in Ron's studio flat on video tape over three nights. It cost £5000 to make, with the funding coming from Greater London Arts and, later, the BFI Production Board. The film was edited on U-Matic and transferred to film for cinema exhibition. It was subsequently screened at the 1985 Edinburgh Film Festival. Unfortunately, we had not realised the implications of the BFI's £1500, which meant that Channel 4 owned the film, and it was shown twice in the first year after Edinburgh to a total audience of some four and a half million people, which is very big for a production of its kind. This proved that there existed a significant audience for a film like *Male Nude*, but the producers were unable to reap any financial benefits from this audience. What we did succeed in demonstrating, however, was that even with a film made at home on a miniscule budget with domestic equipment you can achieve a certain degree of sophistication with careful control. In fact, the 16-mm exhibition version of the film is quite acceptable in normal small art house cinemas without any problems with it.

The first substantial project I worked on with Derek Jarman was *The Angelic Conversation*. When this film was being made Derek Malcolm was running the London Film Festival. It was his first year in charge and we promised to provide him with some films for the festival. We found ourselves short of a film to show and were getting a bit desperate. Derek Jarman was keen to show a reel of *Angelic Conversation* as a work in progress but the BFI, who had put up the money for the project, refused. Fortunately, he was due to visit the Soviet Union as part of a delegation of British film-makers organised by the BFI. I suggested to Derek that he film something while he was there and we could knock up a quick little film. He was dubious about the whole thing but I had a special lead-lined bag for carrying film through customs so it is not destroyed. In the event he got some very interesting footage. He arrived back with ten rolls of Super-8 film. We then set up a studio shoot with friends with some extra finance we had acquired, and the result was *Imagining October* – produced on a budget of £4700.

We subsequently finished *Angelic Conversation* at a cost of £40,000. It was made by a small group of people: Derek, myself, two actors, someone to drive us around, and some more working on post-production. The music was provided by an outfit called Coil. It is a very simple, gentle film, and I am very pleased with it.

Scripts and Things
The issue for me is the problem of trying to get films made. It seemed to me that, from the mid-70s to the early 80s, a great many people were trying to have scripts produced. Lots of scripts written but there seemed to be very little money around for anything that was adventurous in cinema. Obviously, the independents were spurred on by things like the New German Cinema and the work that was being done in France and were looking to make quite exciting films; there did not seem to be much opportunity for having films funded which resulted in quite a few people wasting quite a few years on scripts that were never realised. One of the reasons I have been involved in the type of production I have been describing, which more often than not does not begin with a script, is that it is an alternative to spending considerable time developing a script and trying to raise production finance. So although I like the idea of doing large-budget projects, I think at the same time that it is important to make films continuously, otherwise you can never develop as a film-maker – you just become a writer, and the danger of becoming a writer is that you end up making films for talking heads.

Contrary to the arguments of people like James Park,[3] it seems to me that one of the real problems of the British film industry is that everything is so reliant on literature and on scripts. Scripts are discussed, they are changed around and everybody sticks their oar in, with the result that the actual film that is eventually made seems to be almost inconsequential. I believe that this kind of fussing around in development does nobody any good and seems to favour a cinema that is developed from books and from newspaper cuttings rather than a cinema which comes from a film language. Neither *The Last of Eng-*

56

land nor *The Garden* were scripted. That is not to say that scripts *per se* are not important, only that that is not the only way to do things.

If there is interest in a project it should be based on a treatment idea, and then the production should be given at least some undertaking to go ahead. Unfortunately, I find from my experiences that if you get an idea for an original script and you want to work with a scriptwriter and a director you still only get funded to write the script: you do not get funded to make the film. The actual process of script-writing is still kept separate: it is not part of the actual making of the film, it is like something you do until it has been approved to death and altered by everybody who might possibly in the future give you some money, and at the end of the day you have to go looking for the money rather than somebody saying this is a brilliant idea, let's just get it going, let's find the money and make the film.

The problem with not going through that process and acquiring the large budgets that it takes to make normal commercially released films is that you are often told that your films are substandard, that because they are made on small gauges like Super-8 and 16 mm they are not of the necessary quality required for broadcast television. There is less of a problem with cinema screenings, but people do sometimes pick it out: some of my films have been criticised for not being as sharp or as colourful as they should be. I totally disagree. They might not be that sharp but they are certainly colourful. These people tend to be film industry people; I have never had an audience complain to me that a film was not sharp enough. This, like the absolute necessity for a script, is an orthodoxy which needs to be challenged.

Unorthodox Production Methods and Electronic Cinema
By the time I had finished *The Last of England* – which I believe was as far as we could develop, working in Super-8 and video post-production (this film was shot on Super-8, transferred to video for editing and post-production and then transferred back to 35-mm film for cinema exhibition), with the technology available at that time – those of us who had worked on these films (including Derek Jarman, cameraman Chris Hughes, editor Peter Cartwright and a small group of actors including Tilda Swinton) had essentially devised an alternative system of film-making. It certainly was not like normal 35-mm production, where you just pick up the phone and it all happens because everybody knows what you are talking about, where you simply say that you want such and such a film stock, such and such a camera, and it all goes down the line very easily.

With our films the process adopted is a direct development from certain experiments of the kinds of film-making done at art college. Ron Peck's production, *Strip Jack Naked*, funded by the BFI, is a feature-length documentary which is made using simple domestic equipment and domestic-sized resources but yet making something which is of instant interest to an international audience – hence its selection for the Berlin Film Festival. I find that quite remarkable, given that there are other pieces of work made in this country which never seem to get an airing here, never mind abroad, which once again underlines the fact that audiences exist for this kind of film-making.

The process by which both *The Last of England* and *The Garden* (perhaps the most visually sophisticated film we have done) were realised is interesting and worth explaining in some detail. Both films were shot on a mixture of formats. In the case of *The Last of England* almost all of the material was shot on Super-8, with the sequences in Derek's flat on 16 mm. In the case of both films, material had been gathered over a protracted period, often with a strong 'home movie' element where only one or two people were involved. This footage was then supplemented by a more structured shoot involving a full crew. For example, the major sequences in *The Last of England* were shot at Millenium Wharf on the Royal Victoria Dock in East London, often involving four Super-8 cameras recording sequences simultaneously. This material was then integrated with other footage, including fragments of Derek's parents' and grandparents' home movies.

The Garden was more varied, mixing a combination of 16 mm, Super-8 and video. There is also quite a lot of blue-screen processing in this film, with backgrounds shot in Super-8 or video and foregrounds on 16 mm in the studio. The shooting process, which took over two years to complete, can be divided into three stages. Firstly, all the ambient material, including backgrounds, landscapes and sequences with Tilda Swinton as the beachcomber, were shot in Dungeness, London and other locations over a long period before it was decided to make the film as such. This material was shot on Super-8 or video because we have the cameras and it does not cost too much. Secondly, in September and November 1989 we had three days on location with the crew and a generator on location in Dungeness. Finally, we had seven days in the studio where we filmed all the blue-screen material. That was obviously the most expensive part of the film, and in some ways the most conventional, although remember that there was no script, even at this stage. There were a series of sequences that we changed from day to day, including material that we shot and subsequently decided not to include in the final film.

What is interesting about this production is that within the structure there was a certain flexibility which allowed a degree of improvisation on the part of the actors, who seemed to respond very positively. They were used to working with scripts, and on this production they were

58

often given the minimum of direction. It is interesting to consider that while Derek Jarman has a very strong personal style (that is to say, he is an extremely distinctive film-maker) his way of working often provides a space where other people can contribute significantly to the whole. What is also interesting as regards *The Garden* is that Derek was in hospital for much of the editing period, and obviously the editing stage in productions like this and *The Last of England* is of crucial importance. Being substantially non-narrative films they need a strong structure which allows the images to 'make sense'. Both films can be described in terms of a visual (and aural) collage, so what you actually find is that the editors have made a significant input in the way that this film has been made and the way that it works structurally.

Video Post-production
I always thought that having spent an apprenticeship making these unusual films in unusual ways I would eventually progress to 'normal' feature film-making. However, I had become more and more interested in the possibilities afforded by developments in video post-production technology. I have been profoundly influenced by experiments with video as a production medium such as Antonioni's *Oberwald Mystery* and by the work that Coppola was doing on the use of electronic images in cinema. These experiments gave us all courage to get to something like *The Last of England* by creating a way of working as much as just finding the small amount of money to make the film. Apart from providing a highly sophisticated and flexible method of editing and applying visual effects to footage generated on Super-8 or 16-mm film, what I believe video post-production can do is make the kind of magic that cinema had in its wonderful Technicolor days. Video post-production technology, which is now digital, is wonderful in that it can deal with a picture perfectly: no information is lost in going from generation to generation. This is, of course, a problem in film in that even with fine-grain emulsions it deteriorates slightly every time you do a process. With digital video, on the other hand, there is no deterioration. It can come down as many generations as you like and you still retain the same sharpness.

In addition, the whole notion of being able to manipulate the image and to create an artificial world becomes possible with video post-production technology. This affords new possibilities which were formerly confined to the realm of big-budget studio productions with their use of optical special effects and illusion such as matte paintings. My particular love is science fiction cinema, fantasy cinema, and, given the technological developments, I am keen to concentrate on this area and see how that can be developed rather than go on with conventional feature film-making as it is at the moment. One old special-effects method I have utilised in conjunction with the new technology is blue screen.

The first time I made use of the blue-screen process was in the mid-80s. I was working with Jo Comino on a documentary which was made for Channel 4 television called *Super Eight*. This project was given to us as a commission by Alan Fountain to provide a context for a series of Super-8 films shown by the Channel. It is quite an interesting little documentary because it covers the whole world: it examines various uses of Super-8 film in different ways in different countries. One experiment we did was to take a shoe box and cut a hole, which became a miniaturised version of a CinemaScope screen at one end, and covered it with tracing paper. On to this we projected a wide-screen Super-8 film, and recorded this with a video camera. We then filmed a man in front of a blue background and combined the two images. To all intents and purposes he is just standing in a huge cinema with a big screen behind him. It looks really effective, and nobody has yet spotted that it was a shoe box: they all think he is standing in somewhere like the Odeon in Leicester Square. I thought that if we can do something that simply, knock it together in an afternoon and not even have to think about it in advance, what could we do if we really put our minds to it. So I started to experiment more and more with blue-screen processes in the work I was doing, and bit by bit I put together a group of people who can actually get this sort of process to work properly.

I subsequently experimented with blue screen on a little music film I did for the Venice Biennale. It was quite an odd experience making that film. The director was the Italian composer Sylvano Bussotti, and it was his first film. However, this did allow us to do a few things that we probably would not have had the chance to do otherwise. We did the blue-screen process on this one just using a piece of cloth painted blue, which did not advance us technologically very much. We subsequently went on and did another project with the Pet Shop Boys which consisted of eight short sequences to be projected as backgrounds that they were to include in the stage show for their mini world concert tour. Some of these sequences were shot again on Super-8 with blue-screen backgrounds with various background material keyed up: one sequence, for example, featured a Spanish dancer shot in the studio against a blue screen, combined with bullfighting images. We blew this film up to 70 mm with Technicolor for projection and were very impressed when we saw it that big.

What I am interested in is using the technical possibilities afforded by video to interfere with a space. Instead of having a set which is fixed, you can actually change the dimension of the space or add bits

60

to it. So if you set up a space where you are filming, part of the space can be concrete, a built set, and part of it can be electronic so that it can change into a different space. It is like having a room that is completely flexible and is in some respects a logical development from the kind of matte and glass shot work that was done in Hollywood cinema, *Gone With the Wind* being a classic example, and on other films such as *Black Narcissus*. The extension of that is to be able to create a completely flexible space, instead of just a rigid space where you can move a camera in a very limited way. I believe that with a fair amount of help from computer graphics we can actually create a flexible and extraordinary space in films, something in which I am very interested in relation to science fiction and which may give an unconventional edge to reality.

In terms of projects, it is my goal to make those kinds of films. I think *The Garden* has proved (and this is a very abstract and a very difficult film, all of which I do not profess to understand) that there is an audience for this kind of adventurous cinema. It should be possible to make movies which are not just costume dramas and which are not just kitchen-sink-type modern stories. I think there is room for a kind of film-making which we do quite well in this country, particularly when you consider people like Carol Reed, Michael Powell, Ken Russell, Julian Temple and Derek Jarman. I think there is a kind of strange English surrealism that permeates the whole history of our cinema. Michael Powell's films are quite surreal and quite odd and they rely on a great deal of trickery; without the resources that cinema had in those days, I think video provides access to those tricks.

Raising the Money
In general, however, the hardest bit is developing the finance for these films and that is what I find really difficult. To give an example, making music promos is easy in that you go to the record company or they come to you and say, 'right, this is the budget, we need x number of minutes of film, this is the song, you make the video', and it is all done, it is a very simple transaction which involves a contract and that is about it. But with a project like *The Garden* it is not just a question of taking time to find the money: once you have shot the thing it still takes an awful lot of time to persuade people that it is a good project to put money into, because it has no script. The film would never have been completed if it was not for the perseverance of Channel 4, who were of great help, and to come extent British Screen, under the guidance of Simon Relph, and certainly ourselves to actually believe that the project would be good.

All the people we approached were shown some still pictures and knew what Derek was capable of. They had the example of *The Last of England* as a kind of guideline as to what might happen. But they still had great difficulty in being able to imagine the end product or at least to communicate to the other people with whom they were working. For example, a French European satellite company, having been given a presentation by ourselves of the material shot to date, plus stills, plus other bits and pieces, were very excited by the project and were keen to get involved with it. But when it went to their panel for a decision the panel just could not grasp the nature of the project, could not understand why there was no script.

That is the problem: films like this are difficult for people in funding bodies or in financing positions to put money into because there is no script, because there is no written word. At the same time, if you approached any of these people with the idea of making a film like *The Garden*, the chances of getting development to do a script are very limited. So the only reason that most of these films, apart from the music ones, exist is because they have been largely self-financed in the early stages of production. For example, we funded the shoot on *The Last of England* with the money we received from various pop promos. It would be nice to think that with the success of *The Garden* that might change and it would be possible to take on other projects and have them financed. But there is still a reluctance to give any kind of financial undertaking to something which is in any way unconventional. I am still trying to find a way around that and make something a bit more exciting.

However, if it was not for the Pet Shop Boys there would be no film called *The Garden*. The money that Derek and I earned out of doing that film is negligible for the two years of work that went into it, whereas projects like the Pet Shop Boys obviously makes it easier to pay the bills at the end of the day. However, these films also give you an opportunity to develop certain ideas and try certain techniques, the extensive blue-screen work in *The Garden* being a direct development from the experiments done on the Pet Shop Boys' material, for example.

I do not really know where to go to get money in Britain. I feel that in some ways I am more and more drawn to other parts of Europe, being Scottish-Italian by birth, where I find much more enthusiasm and certainly more interest in the areas of work that I am interested in. In fact, the first project I was involved in – making it possible to distribute one of Derek Jarman's early Super-8 films, *In the Shadow of the Sun* – involved European funding, in this case from Germany. I get more and more disillusioned with London and the fact that it does not matter what area your ideas rest in; we have a fairly broad range of projects, but there is so little interest that it is amazing, like beating your head against a brick wall. There is a related problem, and that is a certain resistance from the film establishment to this kind of film-making which does not fit the prevailing American model of production which is so dominant in this country. Such unorthodox productions do not quite fit the bill of what a 'British film' should be. But this is nothing new, as British Film Year demonstrated. As Alexander Walker pointed out, the selection of films chosen to represent British cinema did not include such 'uncomfortable' productions as *Jubilee, Babylon* and *The Ploughman's Lunch*.[4]

Possibilities for the Future

I am not sure how to sum up these possibilities, but I would have hoped that we could have looked at the technological and financial potential afforded by high-definition European video production, though that looks as though it has been blown away for the time begin with the BSB/Sky merger. It is therefore hard to tell how to go forward easily, but I certainly see it as a European thing and that maybe it might be more interesting to work in other parts of Europe rather than work here. I do not see any initiative on the part of the people who are making the normal sort of films to put any money into the kind of production I am involved with. I see no particular concern by the BBC or Channel 4 to finance this kind of film-making in terms of prebuying or even equity finance, and I think that the small amounts that people like British Screen would bring to this kind of film-making are really laughable. I think there would be more chance of developing these notions in places like France, Spain or Italy than here. The BFI does a certain amount of work but it is obviously very limited in its ability to finance projects.

On the technical side I feel that there is a need for a European funding umbrella for small post-production companies, for the current situation is that there are several small post-production facilities struggling to survive. In terms of the technical requirements of the productions I have been involved with I find that company A is competent at a particular service while company B is better in another capacity. Because they need the work, however, company A will promise to undertake both services and produce substandard results compared with company B. What these companies need is to be given the protection to allow them to develop ideas and to collaborate without the fear that they will go out of business tomorrow, or that some conglomerate will swallow them up or exploit them. There are a great many innovative people around who do not have the infrastructure around them to allow them to develop the confidence they need in order to benefit the industry. In some ways this mirrors the problems and the insecurities faced by the small independent producer in this industry.

63

Notes

1. Simon Relph and Jane Headland, *The View From Downing Street* (London: BFI, 1991), p. 6.
2. Simon Perry interviewed by Oscar Moore, *Screen International*, 1 March 1991.
3. See 'False Starts', *Sight and Sound*, Summer 1990, and *British Cinema: The Lights that Failed* (London: Batsford, 1990).
4. Alexander Walker, *National Heroes* (London: Harrap, 1985), p. 270.

PRODUCTION STRATEGIES IN THE UK

Stephen Romer

This paper uses the case study method to explore the supply side of the British film production business. It examines, with reference to five recent films, the methods of raising production finance and the techniques of cost control which are necessary to enable the film to be made within its budgetary constraints.

The five case studies were all carried out in the late 1980s and are as follows:

1. *Buster*, Norma Heyman;
2. *Distant Voices, Still Lives*, British Film Institute;
3. *High Hopes*, Victor Glynn and Simon Channing-Williams;
4. *A World Apart*, Working Title;
5. *A Fish Called Wanda*, Prominent Features.

These examples embrace a diverse range of budgets and funding strategies.

Buster

Buster was the most independent of independent productions. Norma Heyman, the producer, had the idea of setting up the finance along the lines of that of an earlier film, *The Honorary Consul*. This model involved preselling the film not on a world rights basis but territory by territory, the aim being that if the film failed commercially in the USA it would still be possible to make money elsewhere.

Of the target figure of $5.6 million, Heyman attempted to raise $3 million from the USA and the remainder from the rest of the world.

But *Buster* turned out to be a very difficult film to finance. It was turned down for financing in the UK at an early stage. Norma Heyman tried to finance the film at Cannes. Many bankers and sales agents were approached, and (in typical Cannes fashion) a party was thrown. But various potential deals, including one important video interest, ultimately fell through.

Eventually Hemdale bought the US rights for $3 million, supplying

65

a letter of credit to facilitate borrowing. This took place through Pierson Heldring and Pierson, the Dutch merchant bank. They bought in the Japanese-owned British bank Guinness Mahon as a 50/50 partner to defray what they perceived as risk. About $400,000 additional finance was required to cover the various costs of bank finance and interest.

The rest of the world was presold territorially through sales agents, resulting in guarantees from distributors in the UK, Australia, Germany, Italy, and so forth. As opposed to the Hemdale letter of credit, the sales agents, on the basis of these territorial guarantees, put in cash.

At a late stage, the budget still needed $600,000 to achieve full financing. A search in the UK for both City equity investment and production company investment proved fruitless. A promised private investment from the USA fell through at the last minute. There may have been concern about the potential popularity of the (very British) subject matter with US audiences.

Buster was finally produced at a final cost of $5,903,000 (about £3.3 million). This was about $300,000 over budget, inclusive of the director's and producer's fees which had been deferred.

Above-the-line costs had been kept down as a result of the lack of any acquisition costs. *Buster* is a film concerning one of the Great Train Robbers, but was not based on any particular book or confession about this enduring episode in British social history.

There were, however, a significant number of costly legal consultations concerning about twenty pages of the script, particularly with respect to the police role and to the position of British Railways. Indeed, the latter refused to extend facilities and the sequence in the film showing the mail train leaving Glasgow was footage from the earlier Great Train Robbery film, Peter Yates's 1967 *Robbery*. The raid itself was shot using the facilities of a private railway line.

An important part of the film deals with Buster Edwards's stay in Mexico following his escape from prison. With cost considerations in mind, it was initially thought better to film in Spain. However, as it turned out, this option would have been no cheaper than to shoot on location in Mexico itself.

The Mexican location was intended to take up two weeks of the total ten-week shoot. However, during this period, film was lost in the laboratory, an insurance claim followed, and the stay had to be extended to three weeks. This raises a general problem of filming on location in that the sacrifice of a controlled environment can lead to unforeseen cost overruns.

Fluctuating exchange rates also caused problems. This was a production which was budgeted in dollars but spending was largely in sterling. At the time the budget was fixed the pound was at $1.58, and when it rose during production (to $1.71) this effectively forced down the operating budget of the film.

This in turn led to some severe cuts. For example, the production designer's budget was reduced to £225,000, and was to include all construction materials, although not labour.

A more fortunate situation followed the designation of an arbitrary £75,000 to the music budget. Given that the star of the film was Phil Collins, an album materialised for which Lamont Dozier was brought in to write songs. The spin-off was very profitable, resulting in three top-ten hits in the USA.

Another film was made, and this was at a cost of only £25,000: a video, *The Making of 'Buster'*. This, like the *Buster* enterprise as a whole, will itself be a profitable venture. However, as a truly independent producer, Heyman stresses that she expects to have to devote a day a week for the next seven years to matters associated with the *Buster* project and related issues of distribution and collection.

Distant Voices, Still Lives

The two parts of this film were made separately. The total budget for the first part, *Distant Voices*, was £285,000 and this sum was voted to the film's maker, Terence Davies, by the British Film Institute's Production Board. The subsequent finance required for *Still Lives* was about £350,000 and this came only in part from the BFI, the bulk being raised from ZDF, the German television station.

This British public sector film therefore had to be supported, as is frequently the case, by supplementary co-production finance. In 1990, for example, the BFI Production Board had only about £1 million to put into production. It received just under £0.5 million from the BFI itself, £450,000 from Channel 4, and £60,000 from other commercial television sources. Co-finance is raised, as with *Still Lives*, or, to take a further example, from the BBC and the American HBO for the 1989 production, *Fellow Traveller*.

The BFI is constrained in practice to participation in the finance of a maximum of about four features per annum. It does, however, have a small advantage in terms of access to a specific sector of the film distribution market as its Distribution Division runs a regional network of cinemas throughout the UK.

The BFI also manages to finance a number of shorts from its own funds, and to commission new directorial and writing talent. It was through this door that *Distant Voices* entered the Production Board. Davies said that his *Trilogy* had been ten years in the making, and yet carried a cost of only £45,000. Following his success with this project at the New Directors' Festival in New York, the BFI commissioned him to develop a script.

This script turned out to be *Distant Voices*, and the finance was then released to make the film. On completion, the BFI wanted it to be distributed, but Davies refused, feeling that a second part, *Still Lives*, should be added.

In this sector, financial constraints are, perhaps, more strongly felt than in any other. However, a showing of *Distant Voices* to influential parties was arranged, with the result that Davies was voted development money by the Board for *Still Lives*. This investment, in turn, attracted the ZDF co-finance, enabling the film to be made.

Even by British standards, *Distant Voices, Still Lives* is a very low-budget film. The production costs of its two parts were £279,600 for *Distant Voices*, and £376,150 for *Still Lives*. With the exception of a single brief sequence, the entire film was made on location rather than in the more expensive environment of a film studio. Although the film was set in Liverpool, the locations were found mostly in London, thereby avoiding the out-of-town hotel and other costs for a production unit on a distant location.

This film was, above all, a personal project of the writer/director Terence Davies, for it concerns his family in Liverpool during the war and post-war periods. Davies found, after a lengthy search, a house in London which would satisfy him as a replica of the original family home.

The hard work on the part of the producer, Jennifer Howarth, and her colleagues must be stressed if one is to comprehend the achievement of making such a film at so low a cost. The production team was prepared to undertake a variety of duties in addition to their normal ones – accountancy and chauffeuring, for example, is not usually the producer's province. Moreover, there was no production manager until fairly late in the project.

The fact that this was a BFI production meant that there were certain facilities available to the production which were not formally costed into the budget, such as stationery, photocopying of scripts, office space, storage space, telephones and editing equipment. When a production manager did eventually join the project, it was a full-time member of the BFI staff.

In addition to providing a form of subsidy to budgeted costs, the BFI's presence behind a low-budget film has another advantage in that experienced industry personnel are sometimes attracted to a BFI film, knowing that it is probably a culturally and artistically worthwhile project with which to be involved.

Distant Voices, Still Lives was a film in which music was central – there is a great deal of singing of music hall songs. When it came to

68

obtaining the numerous musical clearances, Howarth's strategy in this potentially expensive area was to adopt a person-to-person approach and to stress the limited budget and scale of the project. Indeed, at the time of the first negotiations, it was only *Distant Voices* which was being discussed. Moreover, successful negotiation with EMI enabled Howarth to approach other copyright owners and ask for similarly low rates – the so-called 'favoured nation status'.

Pre-production lasted fourteen weeks, a lengthy period which included the discovery of the acceptable London locations. The subsequent shooting periods were five weeks for *Distant Voices* and a mere four weeks for *Still Lives*.

In discussing cost control on *Distant Voices, Still Lives*, the role of Terence Davies must be stressed. As the writer and director, he fine-tuned his script in the pre-production stage, carefully planning each scene in the process. As with cost-conscious film-making anywhere, it is vital to ensure that the script will work before shooting starts.

Davies's careful planning and clarity of conception also meant that he was able to say with certainty exactly when and for how long expensive facilities like, say, crane hire would be required. Finally, it was generally thought that his enthusiasm generated a widely shared feeling of commitment to the project among all concerned.

High Hopes

Costing £1.3 million and thus a rather larger project than *Distant Voices, Still Lives*, Mike Leigh's film *High Hopes* is, as a financial proposition, typical of many small British films produced in the second half of the 80s. It is also an example of the Channel 4/British Screen model of finance. To start with, *High Hopes* looked as if it would be easy to finance. The co-producer, Victor Glynn of Portman Productions, said that when the project came his way, he found that Channel 4 were, despite the absence of a story or script, willing to put up finance of £0.75 million, on the basis of Mike Leigh's track record. This comprised £300,000 licence (to show the film on television) and £450,000 equity investment.

At this time, in 1985, British Screen was about to commence operations, approximately taking over the role of the former NFFC. Despite a degree of initial reluctance concerning this project, British Screen agreed, following some lobbying from the producers, to put up £350,000. Portman Productions would supply the remaining £200,000.

Rehearsals then began, in Blackburn, with a cast of well-known actors, and the project started to get off the ground. Unfortunately, at this point Mike Leigh was taken seriously ill.

When he recovered the producers tried to put the financial package back together, though this was rather difficult as, by this time, all parties were somewhat nervous about any investment they might make. Moreover, Leigh's bad fortune had led to an insurance settlement whereby the project recovered, in full, the £250,000 that had been spent in Blackburn. Consequently, the insurers were reluctant to step into a revived project.

However, the story has a happy ending. As a kind of try-out on his comeback, Mike Leigh made a television short which was promptly nominated for a BAFTA award. It was at this stage that Channel 4 and British Screen agreed to return to the fold once the insurance situation was cleared up. Some five years after it began, *High Hopes* found its way on to the screen.

As regards the costs of production of this project, the film was budgeted at £1.3 million and came in slightly under – at £1,288,695.

Leigh's approach to the making of films and television drama is famously unconventional. His projects begin with a group of actors who have no script or story to start work on. The actors then develop and research a piece in an intensive period of rehearsals, with the story emerging out of this process. As such, it has unfortunately been rare for Leigh to have the opportunity of making a theatrical film, for his *modus operandi* runs contrary to received industry practice and the expectations of financiers who will usually only invest in the commercial potential of a completed script.

However, Victor Glynn, the co-producer of *High Hopes* (with Simon Channing-Williams) was an exception. He was delighted at having the opportunity of producing a film which would mark Leigh's return to the cinema after many years. (His only previous cinema film, *Bleak Moments*, was made in 1971.)

How did Glynn deal with the budgetary side of the situation in such a way as to accommodate Leigh's particular approach? The answer was to take away all known costs from the total budget of £1.3 million. Thus he subtracted the fees of the major personnel, the cost of the completion guarantee and of the contingency reserve. He further identified the costs that would actually be required to make the film: the cost of a crew on the basis of a six-day week for seven weeks was a known quantity, as was, approximately, the cost of twelve weeks for editing.

These subtractions left Glynn with £300,000 to award to Leigh to finance the actors in rehearsal. All the actors were to be paid the same rate, and the £300,000 meant that there were 650 actor weeks at Leigh's disposal. He was free to deploy them as he saw fit – he could, if he wished, rehearse one actor for 650 weeks, or 650 actors for one week, or any combination between these constraints!

In the event, the rehearsals took fifteen weeks. Many actors came

70

and took on the stimulating, if somewhat exacting, assignment of auditioning while not knowing what play they were in, let alone what part they were playing!

Glynn's other major cost-control device was to insist that five minutes' screen time per day should be produced during shooting. That *High Hopes* did come in on budget was, in Glynn's opinion, because Leigh is a very disciplined and hard-working director. Moreover, if the film *did* get behind schedule then, because there was no script as a blueprint to work from, it was not the case that completion of the scene in question would be seen as crucial to the project as a whole.

Needless to say for such a low-budget film, all shooting was on location. It was centred on a council flat hired by the producers in Kings Cross.

A World Apart

Where *High Hopes*, costing less than £1.5 million, can be regarded as belonging to the low-budget category, the planned cost of *A World Apart* of £2.6 million puts it in the medium-budget bracket, namely, between £1.5 and £3 million. This meant that, in addition to relying on Channel 4 and British Screen sources, this project required supplementary sources of finance.

Initial development money was raised in Zimbabwe by the London production company, Working Title, for the carrying out of pre-production research. Once a budget was drawn up, the first stage in raising the necessary £2.6 million was to send the script to British Screen and to various television companies. This was successful to the extent that British Screen agreed to subscribe £0.5 million, and Channel Four offered £0.3 million in exchange for a licence (three transmissions over five years).

There were no takers among the major US studios that were approached. *A World Apart*'s subject matter was apartheid in South Africa, and it was felt that existing projects like *Cry Freedom* and *A Dry White Season* had monopolised what interest was going for this general subject.

However, the mid-80s was a period when the American independent distribution sector was buoyant. Working Title's distributor for an earlier film, *Wish You Were Here*, was the Atlantic Entertainment Group's Atlantic Releasing. They expressed an interest in *A World Apart*, agreeing to buy all North American rights for £1,320,000, just over half the budget. Half of Atlantic's financing was to be paid at the completion of photography, and the remainder in instalments until delivery. In the meantime, Atlantic's practice was, in all probability, to cover their outlay by laying off some of the rights to video distributors.

Working Title raised the actual cash against Atlantic's obligations from the Dutch merchant bank Pierson Heldring and Pierson. This cash plus the British Screen and Channel 4 money still left about £500,000 to be found, and eventually this was forthcoming from a private investor in Zimbabwe.

A World Apart was made for a total final cost of £2,715,000, slightly in excess of its budget of £2,652,000.

The film was photographed during nine weeks on location in Zimbabwe (there was no use of studios) starting in June 1987. This followed eight weeks of pre-production, a period which included extensive tests and rehearsals designed to discover the right actress to play the part of the thirteen-year-old girl at the centre of the film. Post-production lasted a final period of eighteen weeks.

For the co-executive producer of A World Apart, Tim Bevan, above-the-line costs, at about 10 per cent of budget, were remarkably low. He felt that the services of the writer, Shawn Slovo, and of the American star, Barbara Hershey, were obtained on very favourable terms.

An eminent technical crew was secured at fees which were low relative to market rates. Personnel were attracted by an affinity with the work of Chris Menges, the celebrated British cinematographer, for whom A World Apart was his directorial debut.

The main area in which this film went over its budget, however, was in post-production. The contingency had already been spent and there was little room for manoeuvre on music and cutting, and so on. Editing costs, for example, were some £40,000 over budget.

A Fish Called Wanda

With A Fish Called Wanda, which was budgeted at $7.3 million (about £4.5 million), we move into the sphere of the larger-budget film, those with costs in excess of £3 million. This film's finance was raised entirely in Hollywood – it was a British film financed by a major studio (MGM).

The project originated from John Cleese who wrote the script, acted the leading role, informally co-directed (with Charles Crichton), and became co-executive producer with Steve Abbot. Cleese's objective was to retain complete overall control of the project. To this end, in the period before the film's production company, Prominent Features, was formed, Cleese himself financed the development phase. Although the opportunity cost of his input may have been high during this two-year period, the monetary outgoings (covering the drawing up of the budget, flying in the principals for script meetings, and so on) were no more than about £20,000.

Abbot said that the strategy was to have all key aspects of the project in place before approaching the majors for finance. The leading players were secured; the script had been developed for two years; and production schedules had been thoroughly planned. In the event, when the producers did go to Hollywood, submitting the project to both MGM and Universal, Alan Ladd Jnr offered the $7.3 million without even seeing the script! The only conditions imposed by MGM were the right to approve the film's designer, editor and production manager.

The deal involved MGM having world rights, including television. Rather than a pure gross percentage (which requires a remarkable degree of bargaining power), Prominent would obtain a percentage of gross revenues at certain trigger points based on multiples of the negative cost. This negotiation on profit participation was conducted in such a way as to attempt a balance whereby MGM would be encouraged to invest in distribution.

This case raises the issue of obtaining production finance from the Hollywood majors. Clearly a track record (such as that of Cleese himself, and association with the *Monty Python* films) will facilitate an interview in the studios with important decision-makers in the production sector. There is, however, a production/marketing interface, and it is important that the marketing decision-makers, who will not have seen the producer's presentation, have some key names to react to (in this case, the American actors Jamie Lee Curtis and Kevin Kline).

As is well known, the rate of turnover of studio executives is rapid, and a consequent danger of this form of finance is that the gestation of a studio film may be rather longer than the average tenure of a studio executive! Furthermore, the ownership of studios can change hands, as MGM's almost did during this period, a change which might have jeopardised the film's release.

The producers felt that if the above-the-line costs were kept as low as possible, this would maximise the chance of the film's financiers keeping to the kind of arm's length relationship with the production that they sought. This was their major objective. Hence, the film's four stars (Cleese, Michael Palin, Curtis and Kline) were signed for well below market rates, but with profit participation points. The budget would have been perhaps $9 million, rather than $7.3 million, had Hollywood salaries been paid. In the event, above-the-line costs were approximately £2 million.

Such a budget is far from small by the standards of British film-making, and this allowed for a degree of relative luxury: an approximate 50/50 division between location and studio shooting. The film was shot, using an entirely British crew, in ten weeks. These were five-day weeks, in consideration, among other things, of the seniority of age of the director, the Ealing comedies' veteran Charles Crichton.

A completion guarantee was not required as such, but the producers' and director's fees were deferred against the possibility of the film being more than 10 per cent over budget. A bonus was paid for delivery on time.

Although certain cost categories were over budget, the largest being music, *A Fish Called Wanda* came in some $300,000 under budget. After test marketing in the USA, this money was used for some re-shooting designed to make the film less bloody and generally more user friendly!

Conclusions

In the contemporary environment of the film industry, British film-makers are likely to face enormous obstacles in raising production finance. If they succeed, it is probable that the budget will have been pared down to well below £3 million.

Consigned to small budgets (if they can be raised), the film-maker faces a quotidian struggle for cost control. Terence Davies, in the case of *Distant Voices, Still Lives*, provides a model of efficiency through extreme care in the preparation of script and schedule.

For *High Hopes*, Victor Glynn and Mike Leigh originally intended a much larger-scale production which would perhaps have enabled more effective competition in the international arena. Glynn approached every conceivable finance source but without luck. The only response he was able to report was that of Messrs Golan and Globus from Cannon Films who offered $100,000 for the world distribution rights!

Yet even the finance sources which they fell back on and which have sustained a low-budget British sector in recent years remain uncertain. The future of British Screen is by no means guaranteed, while the boom in television investment in feature films seems to have come and gone. The real value of Channel 4's contribution has waned, while the commercial television sector generally retreated from the film scene in the build-up to the franchise bids.

The medium-budget *A World Apart* supplemented these finance sources by selling half the budget against North American rights. Of this model, it is worth noting that the presale to the American distributor leaves the fate of the film in the USA at the mercy of the amount of marketing the distributor decides to undertake. In the case of *A World Apart*, Atlantic (in financial difficulties) did relatively little marketing, with the resulting underperformance of the film.

Furthermore, preselling is an expensive method of film finance in terms of the costs imposed by banks for contract discounting. In the case of *Buster*, about $400,000 was required to cover the various costs of bank financing and interest.

74

Other things being equal, it is ideal in distribution to have the weight of a major behind a film, as with *A Fish Called Wanda*.

But with *A World Apart*, no major would get involved in the first place. The US independent distribution sector has been extremely volatile in recent years, and, shortly after *A World Apart*, Atlantic Releasing did indeed go out of business (in June 1989).

It is interesting to note the nationality of finance. Taking Working Title as an example, in addition to *A World Apart*, their successes include *My Beautiful Laundrette*, *Personal Services*, and *Wish You Were Here*. Totally British finance sources have usually been limited to British Screen and television companies, primarily Channel 4. Piersons is a Dutch merchant bank and Working Title's corporate investor is also Dutch. This sort of position, which has deteriorated over the last five years, means that even in cases where there is profitability, money does not come back to the UK film-financing scene.

Note

These case studies were based on interviews with the following:

Steve Abbott of Prominent Studios, executive producer of *A Fish Called Wanda*;

Tim Bevan and Graham Bradstreet of Working Title, executive producers of *A World Apart*;

Terence Davies, writer and director of *Distant Voices, Still Lives*;

Victor Glynn of Portman Productions, co-producer of *High Hopes*;

Norma Heyman of Buster Productions, producer of *Buster*;

Jennifer Howarth, producer of *Distant Voices, Still Lives*.

INDEPENDENT DISTRIBUTION IN THE UK
Problems and Proposals

Julian Petley

One of the many reasons why it is so difficult to raise production finance for a British film is that once the monies have been found and the film actually made (both fraught enough processes in themselves) there are yet more problems to be faced, this time in the interconnected sectors of distribution and exhibition. Difficulties in finding a distributor (let alone one who will handle the film sympathetically), costly delays waiting for vacant screens, the vagaries (to put it politely) of West End exhibition practices, an uncommitted critical climate – all these factors, and more, are enough to make any potential investor wonder whether it is really worth the risk of investing in a production in the first place.

What happens in production, then, is at least partly dependent on what happens in distribution and exhibition. More specifically, it might be argued that the fate of *British* production is closely linked to the state of *independent* distribution and, to a lesser extent, exhibition. In what follows I want to examine some of the problems facing independent distributors in the UK at the moment, and to outline some of the remedies which have been proposed. It is obviously impossible to discuss distribution without touching on aspects of exhibition as well, and I also want to bring in the critical climate in which the films that are exhibited and distributed are received and marketed. My intention is certainly not to present any definitive answers or solutions, but merely to air certain proposals which have been put forward and to hope that these will serve as a useful basis for discussion of an area which still tends to be overlooked when the state of British cinema is on the agenda.

The *Screen International* 1990 UK Top 70 chart showed that the five major distributors, namely Warners, Rank, 20th Century-Fox, Columbia Tri-Star and UIP (who distribute films from Paramount, Universal and MGM/UA) were responsible for eighteen out of the top twenty films. The Total Gross of all the major distributors is shown in **Table 1**:

76

Table 1 Distributors' Market Shares

Distributor	Number of Films	Total Gross
Warner Bros	19	£70 453 860
UIP	17	£74 118 061
Columbia Tri-Star	7	£25 319 000
Palace	5	£13 858 900
20th Century-Fox	4	£13 157 108
Rank	6	£10 202 808
Guild	4	£10 768 929

Based on *Moving Pictures International*'s Top 100 the top seven distributors are ranked as follows: UIP, Warner, Columbia Tri-Star, Palace, 20th Century-Fox, Guild, and Rank. (One might note in passing, however, that there are certain slight discrepancies between the *Screen International* Top 70 chart, and the Top 100 published by *Moving Pictures International*, even though both cover the same period, namely 1 December 1989 to 30 November 1990. This once again underlines the urgent need for official statistics to be compiled for the film industry on a statutory basis.)

British films in the *Screen International* chart were *The Krays* (Rank, 22), *Nuns on the Run* (Palace, 27), *All Dogs Go to Heaven* (Rank, 43), *Wilt* (Rank, 51, though the previous year's 27). After this one has to turn to the *Moving Pictures International* chart to find: *My Left Foot* (Palace, 73, though 65 in the previous year's *Screen* chart), *Dancin' Thru' the Dark* (Palace, 85), *The Big Man* (a big disappointment for Palace, 98), and *Hardware* (Palace, 99). One might also note the perennial confusion about what actually *is* a British film anyway. According to some sources, *Shirley Valentine* (UIP, 11), *Memphis Belle* (Warner, 17), and *The Witches* (Warner, 34) are all British, but according to others they are not.

Also of interest for our purposes is the presence of a number of foreign-language films in the charts. These are: *Cinema Paradiso* (Palace, 48), *Trop belle pour toi* (Artificial Eye, 62), *Tie Me Up! Tie Me Down!* (Enterprise 66), *Nikita* (Palace, 82), *Monsieur Hire* (Palace, 92), *Milou in May* (Gala/Curzon, 95), and *Romuald and Juliette* (Gala/Curzon, 100).

For all their slight disparities, the two charts do indeed demonstrate that the five major distributors dominate the market. This, however, is hardly very startling. More to the point, perhaps, they show the enormous financial gulf between even the top two positions (a clear demonstration of the blockbuster phenomenon), while the table above points up the vast disparity between Warners/UIP and all the rest. On the other hand, we need to note the presence of two independents here – Palace, thanks in no small part to *When Harry Met Sally* (10), and Guild with *Total Recall* (5). It also becomes clear that when it comes to the distribution of non-mainstream Hollywood product the independents play an absolutely crucial role. Many of them, though, account in terms of market share for less than one per cent of even the top 100. Furthermore, the presence of the British and foreign-language films in the chart has to be read against the total numbers brought into distribution in the period in question. Working from the 1990 *Monthly Film Bulletin* one discovers that in 1990 there were 26 UK productions, 5 in which the UK was involved as a co-production partner, 47 subtitled films (of which 3 were reissues), and 8 'English-language versions' of European films. In other words, those British or other European films which make it even into the top 100 are only a small proportion of the totals on offer. One might also note that the films in that chart come from a total of only 14 distributors, while under the heading of 'Distributors: Theatrical' the 1991 *BFI Handbook* lists 64 and the 1990–1 *Screen Yearbook* lists 113. Significantly, perhaps, three of the fourteen (Enterprise, Medusa and Oasis) are no longer trading as distributors.

The example of Guild, in particular, suggests that before we go any further we need at least a working definition of the term 'independent'. Like 'democracy' and 'freedom' this has come to be used in a pretty elastic and promiscuous fashion, as in independent television (that television which does not emanate from the BBC), independent producer, and independent film-maker in the radical, workshop/co-op sense. When applied to the distribution sector the word 'independent' has usually been taken to denote that the distributor in question is not tied to the products of any particular Hollywood studio, but I would suggest that the definition needs to be expanded to cover the *kinds* of film distributed and to include a commitment to British cinema, Europe, the Third World, and left-field Hollywood as well. One also needs to distinguish between those independents who are fortunate enough to have their own cinemas (for example, Artificial Eye, Mainline and Metro) and those who are wholly dependent on other exhibitors to show their product (such as Blue Dolphin).

There have been few thorough surveys of the independent distribution and exhibition sectors in Britain over the past few years. The most useful work is contained in the 1983 Monopolies and Mergers Commission *Report on the Supply of Films for Exhibition in Cinemas*,[1] the chapter entitled 'Distributing the Product' by Archie Tait in *British Cinema Now*,[2] and the section on the UK in volume 2 of the 1988 EFDO report, *Distribution and Export of Low-budget Films in the European Community Countries* (this section was also written by Archie Tait).[3] Before going any further, it might be worth trying to summarise the relevant parts of these documents.

According to the Association of Independent Producers (now merged with the British Film and Television Producers Association, which itself may soon merge with the Independent Programme Producers Association) in the MMC report, the main problems lay with the major exhibitors, then Rank and EMI. Their practice of holding a large amount of product for extended runs at their metropolitan multi-screen centres had worked to the detriment of other exhibitors, many of whom had been pushed out of business. Rather than use their new screens to try to appeal to those other than the 16–25 age group they had consistently neglected 'the more diverse and sophisticated tastes of other sectors of the potential audience'. Through adherence to the system of 'alignments' (whereby, in today's terms, Rank gets first choice on Columbia, Fox, Disney/Touchstone and United Artists films and Cannon is offered Universal, Paramount and Warner) they had been more than happy to accept and encourage the American domination of the British market. It was also felt that exhibitors encouraged distributors to spend most of their promotional budgets in London, thereby leaving little for the regions. The system of dividing up the box office take between distributor and exhibitor (and especially the unilateral imposition of break figures) was felt to be unfair because it ensured that it was the independent distributor who was forced to bear the substantial part of the loss on unsuccessful films. Barring practices (exclusivity agreements between the major distributors and exhibitors) effectively excluded profitable new releases from independent cinemas until they were largely played out, and prevented distributors from working out the best patterns for the release of particular films. Flexibility was also inhibited by the centralised booking practices of the major circuits, and the Association argued for 'more local autonomy in decision-making and a choice of product which was more varied and better attuned to the preferences of local audiences'.

The views of the distributors tended to vary according to whether they were members of the Society of Film Distributors (the main distributors' body, which includes the majors) or independents. Hardly surprisingly, it was the latter who were most critical of the system, complaining that some of the major exhibitors gave preferential terms to members of the SFD. Others remarked that:

> the offerings of the major distributors took precedence over product from smaller distributors, irrespective of quality. The great number of new releases and reissues from the major distributors, and the many hold-overs, caused a pile-up of independent films waiting to

be dated. A circuit might be willing to date a film when the opportunity arose, but bookings were frequently deferred at short notice; this made any kind of business prediction impossible and created difficulties in planning advertising and publicity.[4]

The Association of Independent Cinemas (now, significantly, merged with the Cinema Exhibitors' Association) also complained about bars and the allocation of product, and the distributors' practice of booking certain major films at higher-than-normal rates of hire, which frequently meant that 'small independent exhibitors could not make enough profit from showing these films to cover the cost of exhibiting the less successful films which formed the major parts of their programmes'. Individual independent exhibitors also criticised the minimum playing times sometimes demanded by distributors for the most popular films, and 'problems in negotiating increases in break figures to preserve the exhibitor's share of the box office in an inflationary situation'.

The British Film Institute, in its submission to the MMC, noted that the spread of multi-screen cinemas had not led to a diversification of the films on offer, as had once been hoped. Instead,

the holding over of successful films beyond their initial booking resulted, on the one hand, in a log-jam in the release of new titles, which tended to frustrate the efforts of smaller distributors, and on the other hand in delays in the release of films for second and subsequent runs at independent cinemas. Expenditure on publicity and launch promotion by the major distributors was often very high, and this operated to the inadvertent disadvantage of smaller distributors, tending to influence independent cinemas to compete for subsequent runs of circuit films, instead of diversifying into other, less familiar kinds of film.[5]

It was also felt that present trade structures made it difficult to meet the growing need for specialised marketing caused by the increasing fragmentation of the market into 'distinct, non-overlapping interest groups'. This lack of flexibility 'resulted in films not being shown which, if marketed appropriately, could well be profitable, or at least could develop new sectors within the market, e.g., for foreign-language and classic films'.

The National Film Finance Corporation (disbanded by the government in 1985) made the crucial point that one of the reasons why it was so difficult for British films to attract production finance was the weak competitive position of those films in the exhibition sector, adding that:

booking decisions often appeared to be related less to potential or performance than to dates available and to gaps in the torrent of American product. Distributors were informed very late, and often not informed at all, about films being moved or held over, exacerbating an already difficult situation with advertisement deadlines ... The few indigenous films which were still being made often did not fulfil their potential because of the booking policies of the circuits, and because distributors were disinclined to take the risk of spending the large sums needed for publicity.[6]

Among the remedies proposed by the various independents who submitted evidence to the MMC were a code of practice which would protect the rights of independent exhibitors, an independent body to which exhibitors could appeal if they felt they were being treated unfairly, a relaxation of barring practices, measures to prevent cinemas from holding over successful films for weeks on end, the control of higher than normal film hire rates and of distributors' ability to impose minimum playing times, and an independent procedure for dealing with disputes between distributors and exhibitors over terms. The NFFC proposed

(a) a franchise system under which local independent exhibitors would be given the franchise to run some of the cinemas owned by the major circuits, adhering to the Rank or EMI booking policies for certain periods or films, but otherwise being free to adopt booking policies which were relevant to the area and based on the exhibitor's knowledge of local audience taste; and (b) a more flexible use of the multiplexes by enabling an independent exhibitor to lease one of the screens in a complex.[7]

The BFI, meanwhile, took a broad view of the issues, arguing that:

a number of steps should be taken to promote new thinking and practices in the industry. In particular, there was a need to promote practices in distribution and exhibition which would recognise the needs of specialised films and the appropriate marketing of them. This would require greater variation in release patterns and publicity campaigns, and new forms of liaison between the commercial and cultural sectors, and with television. . . . Greater flexibility in allocation of product should be sought, recognising that different films suited different cinemas, and arrangements should be made to give independent distributors better access to circuit cinemas, particularly where these were the only cinemas within a large area.[8]

In his contribution to the 1988 EFDO report, Archie Tait noted certain additional problems facing independent distributors and exhibitors, especially those dealing with non-English-language films. The first of these has to do with the determining role of television for, as Tait points out,

> ultimately foreign-language film distributors depend on television sales to underwrite the risk of the theatrical release of their films and ... it is worth observing that without at least the strong chance of a television sale for a film, a distributor is unlikely to take it for distribution.

This point is discussed at greater length in my article 'Where Have the Foreign Films Gone?'[9] from which it is perhaps worth quoting Derek Malcolm's remark that

> if people will now show foreign films only if TV is interested in them, then the real arbiters of what we see on our cinema screens are the people in charge of film buying at Channel 4 and BBC2. And they, of course, are thinking more about their audience ratings than about the state of specialised exhibition.

This is perhaps an appropriate place to note that, with the advent of Channel 4, independent distributors felt that a welcome element of competition had been introduced into the television arena, and that, with Channel 4 and BBC2 bidding for non-English-language films, prices might actually rise. (Even so, one independent complained to me a couple of years ago that he was getting less than one tenth of a penny per head of the TV audience!) Now, the general feeling seems to be that, with so much uncertainty in the TV ecology, the BBC and Channel 4 are cutting back on more 'specialist' acquisitions. Hopes were again raised by the prospect of competition between BSB and Sky, but with the alleged 'merger' these have been dashed, along with BSB's role as a funder of British films. Certainly there can be little to gladden the true independents' heart in the purchasing policies of BSkyB and its apparent lack of interest in home-grown film production. One suggestion, however, is that the television companies should be encouraged (or even obliged) to lengthen their broadcasting hours, and that this space could account for huge amounts of film supply, aimed partly at the time-shift audience. This might not provide a huge income for the independents, but it could none the less prove very useful.

The second major problem identified by Tait has to do with limited print availability. As he points out, distributors of non-English-language films generally expect to recoup their costs and go into profit (where they do) on the London run of their films. If a film is a flop in London it is highly unlikely that it will succeed in the regions. It is rare for a foreign-language film to open at more than three London screens at a time, and the distributor usually buys only a couple of prints, and very rarely more than four. Since regional cinemas depend on playing titles partly on the back of the publicity generated by their London release, and since regional film theatres publish monthly or bimonthly programme booklets, thereby necessitating considerable advance booking of prints, the situation can arise in which unexpectedly popular films have to be pulled from their London run to meet regional booking commitments. Tait also notes that in the regions

a successful film may come off while still playing to packed houses because of the pre-planned programme, and because of limited print availability may not be booked again until several months later, when its popularity may be superseded by more recent releases.[10]

Tait identifies two remedies for the problems which he outlines. The first would entail television paying higher prices for the movies which it screens – *all* of them, not merely independent product of one kind or another. Secondly, he calls for an aid fund for the specialist distributor

which will subsidise selected releases to agreed limits for prints, subtitling and advertising and publicity costs. The fund should be revolving, in the same way as the BFI's distribution aid budget. The film's income after opening should be split between distributor, producer and the aid fund, until the sum advanced by the fund is recouped. The split is then between distributor and producer. The aid fund should not seek to participate in success, only to underwrite failure.[11]

Talking to independent producers, distributors and exhibitors today one finds many echoes of their responses to the MMC, though there are differences of emphasis too. Of course, the MMC report came out at a time when cinema audiences were still in steady decline, before the development of multiplexes outside the duopoly, before the impact of Channel 4 had really made itself felt, and before the video revolution had fully got under way. On the other hand, increases in audiences (at the time of writing cinemas have just reported 27.2 million admissions in the first quarter of 1991, the best result for eleven years) may simply indicate that more people than ever are going to see *Ghost*, *Home Alone* and the like. Similarly, rising numbers of screens (1581 at the end of March 1991 compared with 1552 at the end of December

83

1990) does not necessarily mean that a wider variety or larger number of films are now playing across the country. Although the new US-owned exhibition chains have not been absorbed into the system of 'alignments' described earlier, all this means is that they are supported by all the major distributors and are in the main able to show new product as early as the established duopoly. At the end of March 1991 there were 42 multiplex sites comprising 393 screens, but these were playing much the same material as the local Cannon or Odeon: the familiar problem of long hold-overs of popular films is depressingly common, and *Screen Finance* suggested that 'an increasing slice of the multiplex audience is coming from the "cannibalisation" of traditional cinema audiences rather than the attraction of new viewers'[12] or from any attempt to appeal to audiences not catered for by the duopoly. Certainly Peter Trowell of Hemdale feels that the multiplexes have little positive to offer the independent distributor:

> from my own experience as an independent in 1990, I feel that with the advent of multiplexes my company and fellow independents will find it increasingly difficult in 1991 to maintain even the strongest of independent features for more than one or two weeks, because of mounting pressure from the majors.[13]

Trowell returned to the argument later, this time citing specific examples:

> films that do not offer a big name have to fight for screens against unfair odds. The main problem is that you can have a small movie like *Vampire's Kiss* performing well in London and yet you cannot get enough screens around the regions. On the other hand you can get a movie like *Havana*, which nobody wants to see, pushed throughout the country because its distributor [UIP] also owns a chain of multiplexes. In 1991 it is a big achievement if an independent can keep a film on a screen for more than two weeks.[14]

Indeed, even in the West End there is a shortage of screens; the majors are having to pencil in their releases six or eight months in advance if they want to secure the screens of their choice, while independents are finding it ever more difficult to find spaces for their pictures. The Empire and Plaza are virtually the sole preserve of UIP films, while the Warner West End naturally tends to favour Warner releases. This leaves the rest with a choice between Odeon and Cannon, the latter's presence in the West End not being particularly strong in the first-run, flagship category. All the larger companies involved in UK exhibition and distribution have scoured the West End for possible new multiplex sites, but without success. It seems as if cinemas simply do not generate enough revenue to justify the high cost of prime West End sites.

One of the problems which, as we have seen, dominated the thinking of those who submitted evidence to the MMC was barring. This now seems to loom rather less large in independent demonology. Indeed, many now seem to have come round to the view expressed to the MMC by the NFFC that they did not believe that

the formal lifting or modification of barring would necessarily increase free competition because the circuits could continue to operate in the same way by the major distributors insisting on a system which would have the same result, or by justifying each decision on the basis of commercial judgement.

Certainly there are many who now feel that although barring is demographically out of date and eroded by TV release practices, its complete abolition might well result in a more clandestine and arbitrary system, and not necessarily lead to a situation that was any fairer to the independents. Increasingly, then, the question becomes one of trying to improve the lot of the independent distributor and exhibitor rather than one of clipping the wings of the majors, and to do this in the name of increasing the choices open to distributor, exhibitor and spectator alike.

Such a programme has to offer some possibility of increasing the profitability of the independent sector, either by spreading the existing profits around more evenly than at present, or by increasing net returns from the exhibition sector as a whole, or both. One idea that has been floated here has its roots in the French Regional Development Agency; this would involve offering a minimum proportion of prints of new releases to independent exhibitors when the films are still brand new and thus at their most profitable. Another possible measure, which might at least improve distributor-exhibitor relationships, would be the placing of a legal obligation on distributors to specify in all contracts how many times any specific film has (or will have) been shown previously in the same locality. This would clarify exactly what the distributor was guaranteeing the exhibitor. In order to arbitrate these and other related matters it has also been suggested that a broadly based monitoring group should be set up; this could also initiate a much-needed region-by-region review of film supply throughout the UK. In addition, it has been argued that there is a need for a distribution licensing scheme under which information about all films entering UK theatrical distribution would be centrally recorded. This brings us back once again to the perennial point about the crying need for official statistics about the number of films coming into distribution, the number of cinemas and screens in operation, box office receipts and numbers of admissions, and so on. The publication of the British equivalent of the *Ciné-Chiffres* would make some of the abuses of the system suggested by this paper a great deal more difficult to conceal, and would thus be a significant contribution to the cause and process of reform.

The biggest problem facing *all* distributors today is the cost of launching a new release, and especially the cost of advertising, in a limited market-place. Even the majors are not immune. Rank's Fred Turner states that, 'frankly, UK theatrical is a loss leader. It can cost anywhere between £500,000 to £1 million to release a film, and around eight out of ten films do not recoup on prints and advertising'.[15] The cost of advertising is stressed by Maj-Britt Kirchner of Warner: she describes the situation as 'horrendous; particularly when you are looking at using so many different media outlets'. But at least the majors can take advantage of economies of scale, a luxury not available to most of the independents, and certainly not to the smaller ones.

In the area of subtitled films it has been estimated that for every £1 the distributor spends on a film, that film will have to take £4 at the box office. Depending on how much has been spent on the film in the first place it will have to take between £60,000 and £100,000 (bearing in mind that the exhibitor usually takes two-thirds of the box office receipts) if the distributor is to cover the cost of a launch with two prints. A minimum advertising budget would be £5000, but this could rise, in exceptional circumstances, to around £30,000. The various intermediary stages between getting one's hands on a finished print and getting it before the public are often overlooked, but if one considers that these entail British Board of Film Classification fees, poster design and production, the assembling of press packs, the duping of stills, hiring preview theatres, paying for advertising sites in the tube and perhaps hiring the services of a PR company, then it can be seen that the costs of publicity are considerable.

An interesting insight into this whole process is provided by Mark Le Fanu.[16] Taking the example of Electric Pictures' *La Bête humaine*, he shows how it is perfectly possible to notch up £5000 on striking a clean print, importing the film into the country, having subtitles prepared, exporting the film to Belgium to have the subtitles put on (this service not being available in English laboratories), and finally, bringing it back in again. Le Fanu suggests that the three prints of *La Dolce Vita* (a joint distribution venture between Electric and the BFI) cost £6000 each. No wonder, then, that the general view seems to be that a proper launch of a revival (which at least has the advantage over

86

a totally new film of a good deal of ready-made cultural kudos) costs around £20,000. Of course, it is possible to do it for less: *Rocco and his Brothers* was launched for just £4000, which included the advance to the producer (as part of a six-film 'costs-off-the-top' deal), the striking of a new copy, and publicity for a ten-day run at the NFT. To date, according to Le Fanu, it has recovered £3420, of which £1853 is accounted for by the NFT showings. Since 'classics' have, by definition, a long shelf life the film will undoubtedly go into profit: for example, in its four years in distribution, Oasis's re-release of *A Bout de souffle* which cost £20,000 to launch, grossed over £100,000 at the box office, netting the distributors £38,000 (which has to be split with the BBC, who own the rights). *La Dolce Vita* has to date made profits of £55,000 (which have to be split evenly between Electric and the BFI, after the producer has taken his cut), although it has taken *8½*, launched for £6000, two years to break even.

These various figures demonstrate very clearly that, firstly, there is a huge gulf between what the majors (or the large independents like Guild) and the smaller independents can afford to spend on launching a film, and secondly, launch costs, even *comparatively* low ones, are a major headache for the independent distributor. It was partly to solve such problems, on an EC-wide basis, that the EFDO programme was established as part of the MEDIA 92 scheme. The programme's genesis lay in a study which discovered that 80 per cent of the 500 or so films made annually within the EC are produced on a budget of less than 2.25 million ECUs. Of these, 80 per cent never get a cinema release outside their country of origin. The need to encourage the export of such films was enhanced by the awareness that films from outside the EC (mainly, of course, from the United States) have an average market share of 60 per cent, and sometimes more than 80 per cent.

In the original programme, EFDO's form of aid consisted of an interest-free loan of up to 70,000 ECUs to cover the distribution costs of a low-budget film. To be eligible, the film must have been made in the EC and have been taken by distributors in at least three EC countries. Each distributor must cover half the distribution costs and pay back the loan out of income over and above its own expenses. Ten per cent of any profit goes to EFDO as a 'success dividend'. At the time of writing, however, the ceiling for productions has risen to 4.5 million ECUs, taking into account rising production costs and opening up a new area of the cinema distribution market, while the maximum loan has been raised to 100,000 ECUs. To date EFDO has awarded a total of 241 applications to distributors from the 12 member states, plus Austria and Switzerland. This represents 266 cinema launches of 55 European films. British films which have benefited from the scheme are *Distant Voices, Still Lives, Drowning By Numbers, Resurrected, The Dressmaker* and *Queen of Hearts*. Co-productions aided by EFDO in which Britain has been involved are *Berlin Jerusalem* and *Melancholia*, and British distributors who have participated are Electric, ICA, Mainline, Artificial Eye and Metro. It should also be noted that, at the time of writing, the MEDIA programme, now rechristened MEDIA 91–95, has just given the go-ahead to a new project – SOS (Save our Screens) – which is intended to aid independent cinemas throughout the EC.

The success of the EFDO scheme raises the question of whether it could not be supplemented in the UK by a similar scheme aimed solely at encouraging the distribution of British films in this country. Of course, the question arises of where the initial capital would come from. Perhaps it could be raised via a levy on the box office, or on the sale of prerecorded tapes. The proceeds could then be distributed in the form of a loan to aid the launch of films which were to be released with only a limited number of prints. Possibly, certain specified films could be made VAT-exempt for exhibitors, who could then afford terms which were more attractive to distributors. If all else fails, it has been suggested that producers will eventually have to pay a share of the marketing and advertising costs. There are also those involved in distribution who find the EFDO scheme as currently operated too bureaucratic and unwieldy; a suggestion here is that EFDO should allocate lump sums to individual countries and allow the monies to be distributed from within. Since most British films fall into the low-budget category this might indeed have a beneficial effect on their internal distribution.

Another idea, which has recently been floated by Amber Films, is a financial guarantee system which would secure screenings for indigenous products. The plan here would be to try to establish a regular circuit for British films in the UK by manipulating twenty-five screens to ensure a two-week run for such films. This would guarantee a twelve-month run for each production and would be attractive to commercial bankers such as television companies, who would be relieved of many of the scheduling problems they face when involved with cinema product. Wearied by the negative responses they received from distributors over *T. Dan Smith, Seacoal* and *In Fading Light* (in spite of these films' successes in cinemas abroad), Amber are now planning to approach cinemas directly with their next film, *Dream On*, although it has to be said that this novel idea of do-it-yourself distribution is better suited to a permanent structure such as a workshop than a transient, temporary organisation like so many film production companies.

Since British television operates a quota when it comes to imports, maybe the British cinema could be required to follow suit (again, but this time avoiding the pitfalls of previous attempts). Perhaps a Films Bank could be established, offering low-interest loans not simply to production but to independent distribution and exhibition schemes too. This could come within the remit of a British Films Authority, itself answerable to a Ministry of Culture.

Well, of course, we can all dream up wonderful and probably even workable schemes, but if the political will does not exist at government level to see them put into operation and given a chance this may be rather a vain exercise. On the other hand, surely a government which prides itself on introducing measures to increase consumer choice and sovereignty, which has harped on and on about the evils of the 'cosy duopoly' in television, and has actually legislated a quota for the independents on the BBC and Channel 3, cannot be entirely blind to the *de facto* monopoly situation which has been proved (by the MMC report) to exist in the matter of film supply, a situation which undoubtedly works to deny the audience a full range of choice and variety of viewing? So, why not a Twenty-five Per Cent campaign for independent exhibitors and distributors? Or is television some kind of special case?

One of the more encouraging signs in the field of independent distribution recently has been the resurgence of 'specialist' video labels. In the early days of video which were, after all, largely dominated by independents of one kind or another, there were actually quite a few subtitled and otherwise minority-taste videos on the market, then largely dominated by the rental sector. With the passing of the Video Recordings Act, however, and the subsequent need to classify (at no little expense) the entire back catalogue of every single distributor, many of the less popular titles simply dropped out of the market because it was simply not economic to put them through the classification process. However, with the advent of sell-through, the 'art video' seems to be returning in strength – witness the success of Connoisseur Video, and the arrival of Palace and Artificial Eye in this particular sector of the market. However, various caveats have to be entered here. First of all, the major distributors, having shied away from video in its early days, are now consolidating their grip on the business. Concentration is on the increase in all areas of the video business, and the independents' share has begun to shrink.

Secondly, video distributors have not made significant contributions to actual film production in the UK. As Jane Headland and Simon Relph point out,

in spite of the size and relative prosperity of the industry, particularly in the UK, few video companies make direct investments in production, although a number have prepurchased rights. Parkfield Entertainment financed the whole of a major and very successful British production, *The Krays*, before its collapse. . . . It is sometimes possible to secure a pre-production advance against theatrical and video rights in the United Kingdom or a guarantee of revenues from distribution against which another investor may be prepared to lend. Independent British distributors have been particularly ready to support local production in this way.[17]

While this is true, it also leads on to the third point which is that video rental, which is arguably better for the film-making ecology than sell-through, has begun to decline in volume and value in the UK (down about 5 per cent in the first nine months of 1990 compared with the same period in the previous year, according to statistics collated for the British Videogram Association). The problem here is that, in terms of feature films, rental revenue outscores sell-through revenue by about four to one: 'sell-through is a high-volume, low-margin business, while rental is a low-volume, high-margin business',[18] a point which is illustrated by a breakdown of typical video prices.

Table 2   Breakdown of Typical Video Prices

Sell-through
£9.99 – consumer price per cassette

£6.75 – dealer price per cassette
£0.75 – returns, bad debts, discounts
£0.60 – marketing
£2.00 – duplication and packaging
£1.00 – distribution

£2.40 – return to distributor

Rental
£ 1.50 – consumer price per rental

£55.00 – dealer price per cassette
£10.00 – returns, bad debts, discounts
£ 5.00 – marketing
£ 2.00 – duplication and packaging
£ 1.00 – distribution

£37.00 – return to distributor

Screen Finance calculates that a distributor has to sell fifteen times

90

as many sell-through cassettes in order to generate the same returns as one rental cassette, and illustrates the point with the example of a typical rental video which

> might shift 26,000 cassettes at a dealer price of £55 per unit, generating gross revenues of £1.43 million and net revenues of £960,000 for the distributor. This money would be used to repay the original advance to the producer and to contribute to the distributor's overheads. In order to achieve the same level of net revenue for the distributor, the sell-through release would have to achieve sales of about 300,000 units, which would be above average for the UK.

The main point at issue here is that if video revenues decline then independent distributors may (a) feel less inclined to take 'specialist' titles and (b) find that they do not have sufficient capital to become involved in production in any way. On the other hand, of course, it has to be noted that Connoisseur, for one, has aimed itself fairly and squarely at the sell-through sector, and is prospering there.

Finally, it is worth noting that both sell-through *and* rental may be at risk from satellite in the form of BSkyB (who, as we have seen, have not been exactly enthusiastic investors in production of any kind, let alone British or other European films). According to a survey commissioned by *Satellite TV Finance*,[19] subscribers to Sky movies reported significant changes in their video renting and buying practices after becoming subscribers. Thus while 84 per cent of subscribers claimed that they had rented at least one cassette a month before subscribing to Sky, this figure dropped to 31 per cent afterwards. In the sell-through sector 9 per cent of subscribers buy one or more videos a month, compared with a pre-subscription figure of 17 per cent. Members of this group have also cut down on their cinema visits, although it has to be admitted that they were poor cinema-goers in the first place. Of course, these are early and still pretty uncertain days for satellite broadcasting in the UK, but the survey does seem to suggest that satellite movie channels could seriously dent the home-video market.

The final difficulty facing the independent distributor/exhibitor of non-mainstream Hollywood product which I want to consider has to do with the critical climate and audience tastes. These are not necessarily the same thing, and I would also argue that there are different problems here facing the subtitled film and the indigenous one. As far as the former is concerned, most distributors seem to feel that audiences are now far less adventurous in their tastes than they were in the heyday of 'art cinema'. As Andi Engel said to me when I was researching the *Sight and Sound* article:

people have lost much of their curiosity about foreign films. Unless a foreign film is really hyped by the quality press, people just won't come; it has to be a *Babette's Feast* or they don't want to know. For example, compare the fate of *The Commissar* in Germany and the UK; it's not always the fault of the film or of the distributor, but of the society we work in. You can't always say 'it's the wrong cinema' or 'it's the wrong newspaper' – maybe it's just the wrong audience. Foreign films do get coverage in the press, and still people don't come. People don't seem to be interested in finding out for themselves what the films are about any more; they're happy to read about them in the paper and then go off and see the latest Hollywood release. People today seem to lack any cinematic curiosity. I agree that young people are interested in cinema, but not in *that* kind of cinema. But this is like going into a library and deciding that you'll only ever look in one part of it and ignore the rest. That to me is moronic. It doesn't mean that you don't read at all, but it does mean that you're not prepared to consider everything there is on offer, even out of curiosity. That's what I find frightening.

Of course, such sentiments could be dismissed by the cynical as disappointed self-interest masquerading as concern about the state of specialist cinema in the UK, so it is perhaps worth quoting from something which *Time Out* film editor Geoff Andrew wrote to me at the same time:

Distributors and exhibitors do tend to be over-cautious, but then what can you expect in a country where both the government and half the population prize British sovreignty so highly, and where the government remains steadfastly neglectful of a medium it refuses to recognise as an art form? There seems little hope unless there is a complete shift in the everyday attitudes of the average English person towards the cultural values of the rest of the world, and towards the phenomenon of cinema itself. While anything foreign is viewed with caution and suspicion, and while most people continue to regard cinema *purely* as time-passing entertainment, the outlook regarding the distribution and exhibition of non-English-language films seems bleak indeed.

Since these words were written we have also witnessed the depressing spectacle of the demotion of the *Times* film critic David Robinson, allegedly for not paying enough attention to mainstream Hollywood releases in his column.

But if the critics are generally supportive of subtitled films, the same cannot be said of their attitude to the home-grown product, while audiences seem content to wait for new British films to turn up on television. As Gilbert Adair has noted, 'the history of the British cinema is that of an inferiority complex', one which extends to British film critics too. Thus, for example, James Park's book *Learning to Dream* begins with the words, 'the history of the British cinema has been one of unparalleled mediocrity', while one of the few chapters in *British Cinema Now* on the content (as opposed to the producing structures) of new British films is apologetically entitled 'But is it Cinema?' It often seems as if British films are doomed to be disparaged by the critics whatever they do: in spite of the Griersonian legacy, naturalism is simply dismissed as being too televisual (witness the difficulties faced by Amber's *Seacoal* and *In Fading Light* in finding any kind of theatrical distribution), while those who go in the opposite direction, like Philip Ridley with *The Reflecting Skin*, are almost universally criticised for being too 'flashy' (shades of the Powell/Pressburger controversy all over again). No one is, of course, arguing that all British critics should like and recommend every new British film that comes out, but a little consistency and informed debate would be very useful. As Daniel Battsek and Robert Mitchell of Palace complained, 'the British media are constantly calling for home-produced films to have international stars and cinematic appeal. *The Big Man* attempted to introduce an epic style of film-making to a parochial subject matter and was lambasted for it.'[20] Too often, it seems, the mere fact that a film is British condemns it out of hand in our notoriously self-lacerating culture. An end to this negative, masochistic, self-destructive attitude should also be considered as one of the solutions to some of the problems facing the institutions of British cinema.

Notes

I would particularly like to thank Chris Auty, Ian Christie, Barry Edson, Andi Engel, Pamela Hare-Duke, Lori Keating, Murray Martin and Pat McCarthy for their help and advice in preparing this paper.

1. *Films: A Report on the Supply of Films for Exhibition in Cinemas* (London: HMSO, 1983).
2. Martyn Auty and Nick Roddick (eds), *British Cinema Now* (London: BFI, 1985).
3. *Distribution and Exhibition of Low-budget Films in the European Community Countries*, vol. 2 (Hamburg: Hamburger Filmburo, 1988).
4. *Films*, op. cit., p. 46.
5. Ibid., p. 49.
6. Ibid., p. 50.
7. Ibid., p. 50.
8. Ibid., p. 49.

9. Julian Petley, 'Where Have the Foreign Films Gone?', *Sight and Sound*, Autumn 1989.
10. *Distribution and Exhibition of Low Budget Films*, op. cit., p. 41.
11. Ibid., p. 44.
12. *Screen Finance*, 6 March 1991.
13. *Screen International*, 18 January 1991.
14. *Screen International*, 22 March 1991.
15. *Moving Pictures International*, 4 January 1991.
16. Mark Le Fanu, 'Classic Revivals Offer Modest Profits', *Screen Finance*, 1 May 1991.
17. Jane Headland and Simon Relph, *The View From Downing Street*, UK Film Initiatives 1 (London: BFI, 1991).
18. *Screen Finance*, 29 November 1990.
19. Reported in *Screen Finance*, 17 April 1991.
20. *Screen International*, 18 January 1991.

MARKETING ISSUES IN THE FILM INDUSTRY TODAY

James Paul Roberts

The Academic Context

It has long been suggested that the film industry, with its particular structural and procedural characteristics, combined with the apparently unique nature of its product, makes analysis of that industry from a standard business perspective difficult, if not impossible. This difficulty is in turn compounded by the fact that there has never really been an industry-wide information-gathering infrastructure, generating information to aid decision-making practitioners and analysis by academics. This problem has clearly become particularly acute since the demise of the Eady levy and with the Department of Trade's waning interest in the industry.

The academic work that has been done in the industry has thus tended to avoid the business-related issues and concentrate on subjective debates about the aesthetic qualities of film or analysing film as a model of communication.

It is now becoming clear, however, that the industry does share a number of significant structural, procedural and product characteristics with other industries, and as such can benefit from the academic and practical work that has been done in other commercial sectors.

Bearing in mind the present state of the British industry, the general lack of empirically based academic analysis of the industry that exists, and the developments that have been made over the last twenty years in the disciplines of marketing (particularly service marketing) and business studies, it is perhaps time to attempt to re-evaluate the industry from a business perspective using the tools, techniques, concepts and models that have been developed and refined in recent years.

In this paper I want to focus on the area of marketing in the British film industry. The proposed hypothesis is that the film industry, like many other industries, has adopted marketing in its most superficial and ineffective form, and that this industry has much to benefit from by adopting a considerably broader view of marketing, one that encompasses all the stages of getting the film product to the final consumer.

95

I would also propose that although the discipline of marketing is no panacea for the British film industry, and may not have all of the answers that it needs, it does prompt some of the right questions, and offers us the vocabulary of tools, techniques, concepts and models to ask them.

The questions I shall attempt to address in this paper are:

- How is marketing currently manifested in the industry?
- Can we establish what marketing is all about in its more complete aspect?
- What benefits can we expect from becoming more marketing orientated as an industry, and can the discipline play a role in addressing the problems that currently beset the British industry?

Firstly, then, how is marketing manifested in the film industry today?

Marketing in the Modern Film Industry
Marketing as Promotion

The first, most obvious, and possibly most significant conclusion one comes to, on examining current literature and practice, is that in the film industry as a whole marketing is usually equated with promotion and, more specifically, with the advertising and PR used to launch a film. This is not unique to the film industry, however, and is a common manifestation of the marketing orientation in firms and industries that have yet to explore the full scope of marketing.

This approach is typical of sales- and production-led companies, which tend to produce the products they want to, in the hope that customers will buy them, or can be persuaded to buy them through advertising and the 'hard sell'. Characteristically in these organisations, marketing is equated with a more formal, structured and co-ordinated approach to advertising and promotion, and as such becoming marketing orientated merely means dedicating part of the organisation exclusively to promotional activities. To all intents and purposes, then, structured and co-ordinated promotion is used as a surrogate for marketing.

The film industry is no exception to this – indeed, it is a prime example of an industry which manifests its commitment to marketing through the size of its total promotional spend, and that spend is indeed huge. By the end of the 80s the average cost of promoting a film in the USA had risen to $9 million, with $6–$8 million being seen as the minimum required promotional spend to launch a major studio release.[1] This would include advertising, and often an extensive PR campaign aimed at the press.

96

This high proportion of costs being spent on promotion is not confined solely to the majors. Boyle[2] has suggested that both independent film companies and the majors alike spend on average 30 per cent of a picture's expected gross on co-operative advertising.

The promotion itself is usually quite limited in scope, most being concentrated around the opening of the film and in the broadcast media, that is, TV, print and billboards. For the UK launch of a film this concentration of effort is even more pronounced, with the majority of promotional expenditure going into a film's West End launch. So, when we see a quote which suggests that 'some recent marketing campaigns have cost as much as twice the negative cost',[3] what we are really saying is that some recent *promotional* campaigns have cost twice as much as the film to produce.

This emphasis on marketing as promotion is reinforced in the few publications that address the issues associated with the business side of film-making. Indeed, we have now reached the stage where the two terms, marketing and promotion, are virtually interchangeable. It was suggested in a report produced on the market for British films that 'the two main components of film marketing are advertising and media coverage'.[4]

The reasons that promotion has come to dominate film marketing are too many and varied to describe in detail here. It is clear, however, that at one level, promotion tends to be the most obvious issue to address if a company wants to become more marketing orientated, in that it can be relatively easily parcelled off as a discrete 'chunk' of company business. At another level, promotion also has a role to play in reducing the perceived risk associated with releasing a film, in that good, co-ordinated promotion has proved to be very successful in increasing the revenue-generating potential of that film.

Yet promotion may not be the most significant element of the film marketing mix. As one Hollywood executive puts it, 'anyone who understands the movie business will agree that movie grosses are achieved 70 per cent by the film itself and 30 per cent by marketing, sales and promotion'.[5] Perhaps, then, the film industry's equation of marketing with promotion is a little short-sighted, and as such the industry as a whole is missing out on much that marketing, in its more complete aspect, has to offer.

The Use and Misuse of Market Research
One of the central tenets of marketing is that it is only through the generation and use in decision-making of hard empirical data about the market (that is, market research) that a company can effectively develop commercial products and tailor them to the requirements of its market. Is there evidence of this type of activity in the film industry?

Certainly, explicit, discrete market research is conducted, although much of this would appear to be used in the development of promotional campaigns.

There have, however, been instances of market research being used in a wider context, specifically in the screening of ideas and the development of film projects. One significant, if rather extreme, example is the Sunn Classic Pictures experience of the late 70s. Essentially, this company succeeded in identifying an unexploited audience segment in the USA and designed film products to suit their viewing needs, using relatively sophisticated marketing and computer techniques, and notching up an enviable record of commercial successes in the process.

Certainly the use of this type of research has not been confined to one American company in the late 70s. The generation of information about the film market and its use in decision-making must, I suspect, be evident, to a lesser or greater extent, in the running of most production, distribution and exhibition companies on both sides of the Atlantic.

Yet we still are in a position in which the majority of films made, distributed and exhibited fail to make a significant return on the capital invested in them. As one authority has suggested, 'it is generally believed that seven out of ten pictures lose money, two out of ten break even, and one is a huge success, or that two out of every three pictures do not generate enough money to pay for the prints or ads'.[6]

Why is this the case? Perhaps research into the film market, and the suitability of one's product offering for specific markets, is just not being done. Perhaps the wrong kind of research is being done, that is, the wrong questions are being asked. Perhaps the research that is being done is being conducted inadequately. Perhaps we may even be in a situation in which 'the reliable and valid results of adequate research are being ignored or misinterpreted'.[7]

This last point is often justified by practitioners within the industry who claim that existing market research and planning techniques are insufficiently applicable to the movie industry to be of any real value, and as such the results of research are usually worthless and perhaps even dangerous if relied upon too heavily. Richard Kahn expressed this feeling quite succinctly:

Motion picture marketing is not a computer science and never will be. Trained judgements, intuitive leaps, good guesses and common sense must remain the hallmarks of motion picture marketing. If we veer from these criteria we're going to be in serious trouble.[8]

This does much to encapsulate the inherited film industry attitude to marketing, which seems to equate it with a set of informal, intuitive and unstructured decision-making guides – intuition, common sense, good guesses.

In response to this, firstly, formal marketing does not advocate that all decisions should be made on the basis of statistics and the workings of a computer program. There will always be a place in marketing for gut feeling and intuition, as these are usually the best source of good ideas. But this must be balanced with a rational and structured approach to decision-making, using empirical evidence to test this intuition. Too much reliance on gut feeling *or* statistics can be fatal. What marketing tries to achieve is a balanced approach.

Secondly, trained judgements are usually formed after making a lot of mistakes, mistakes which the film industry, with the high cost of producing even the most basic commercial film, and particularly the British industry, with its 'cottage industry' structure, may not have the luxury of making in the present economic environment.

Thirdly, common sense is clearly a very subjective thing, with an equally subjective role to play in decision-making. Perhaps the best way to get round this is to attempt to establish a common ground of empirical data which reflects the state of the market as accurately as is possible, and provides a formal and objective basis for decision-making.

There is, however, some justification for the concern expressed by Kahn. Marketing tools, techniques, models and concepts come in a wide variety of forms and can usually play a useful role in the analysis, planning and control of a business if used intelligently. However, these models often make fundamental assumptions about the way in which markets work, the relationship between profit, volume and economies of scale and experience, and position in the product/market life cycle. It is therefore crucial that adequate time is taken to assess their applicability to the specific needs, functions and characteristics of a particular industry. If this is done carefully marketing's tools and models can be a very valuable aid in analysis, planning and decision-making, and should not be lightly or casually dismissed.

Risk Reduction, Audience Images and Formulas
There is evidence of a further manifestation of marketing in the generation and use of audience images in the decision-making process associated with film development and production.

The desire to reduce risk in the movie business has manifested itself in many ways. In terms of the industry's structure, Strick suggests that 'the larger producers would tend towards restrictive practices in an attempt to gain control and establish a degree of oligopolistic control in the market'.[9] There thus appear to be constant strains towards vertical integration and conglomeration in an increasingly global market.

We have also seen a growth in the use of exhibitor guarantees, the saturation release pattern, presale agreements, TV and press advertising, all in an attempt to reduce the risk associated with producing and releasing a film. However, in terms of the present discussion, the most significant risk-reduction technique used by movie-makers is the development and use of audience images.

The concept of the audience image is described by McQuail thus: 'in an attempt to minimise the predictive difficulties, operators of the movie industry are forced to develop a mental image of the anticipated or desired audience'.[10] This audience image becomes, according to Gans, 'a foil, against which the producer "unconsciously tests his product even while creating it"'.[11] These audience images play, according to Jowett and Linton, a very significant role in decision-making during the development and production stages of film-making. Their use (whether explicitly or more commonly implicitly) is designed to reduce uncertainty and risk, and fit decision-making into a reassuringly rational and apparently empirically based framework.

This is typically achieved by reference to a usually imagined aggregation of cinema-goers, who will theoretically share similar satisfactions from the viewing of a movie. The validity of these audience images would, however, appear to be difficult to assess before a movie is released.

This may be because of what Simonet sees as a fundamental problem, that is, 'the inability of respondents [in surveys] to predict reliably their own future actions, [with them] tend[ing] to report as predictions what they wish they had done already or what has in fact satisfied them in the past'.[12] It may, on the other hand, be that the industry has yet to develop or adopt the techniques and models that would allow this type of analysis of audience images to be undertaken. It may be because of a certain reluctance on the part of executives to make their assumptions about the market explicit and to test them. They do, after all, have much to lose: 'status in the industry depends upon how successful previous decisions [based upon these audience images] have been'.[13]

Whatever the reason, it would appear that, in the main, these audience images are not thoroughly empirically tested before a film is made. Their validity is assumed before a film is released and then assessed after a film is exhibited, based upon its success or failure with the public.

If the film is a success, this can be interpreted by the economic sectors of the industry as being the result of a set of decisions on the part of the executives involved in its production, based upon accurate, valid and appropriate audience images. The audience images of the executives involved take on the aspects of intellectual property, a very valuable and seemingly intuitive grasp of what the public wants, combined with the ability to exploit it.

These audience images often remain internalised in the executive's mind, and emerge in the form of the 'trained judgements, intuitive leaps, good guesses and common sense' that drive much of the decision-making process associated with film-making. Ultimately, a producer, director or writer is employed for the audience image he carries with him, and for his skill in developing film products for this expected or desired audience.

Yet ultimately, this often unquestioning reliance on the apparently axiomatic accuracy and appropriateness of an audience image leads to a situation in which, as Jowett and Linton put it,

> despite the rhetoric of giving people what they want, movie-makers establish the parameters of choice by determining the types of movies that will be produced, and this range of choice is conditioned by a conception of audience preferences that is based upon a set of beliefs that generally lacks empirical support.[14]

Thus decisions are made 'on the basis of irrelevant but enforceable criteria'.[15]

These self-imposed 'parameters of choice' inevitably result in ritualism. This ritualism is manifested both in terms of the people used to create movies and in a routine reliance on formulas and genres that have been successful in the past and in other media. Thus, 'this audience image has tended to narrow the range of subject matter and forms that movies employ, and has caused movie-makers to invoke formulaic approaches and engage in imitations of "breakthrough successes"'.[16]

Often this reliance on formulas brings box office success. Equally, perfectly composed formula films regularly fall flat. The problem may not be the formula itself, but rather the accuracy and applicability of the audience image upon which it is based. Markets always change faster than the companies that serve them, and this is as true of the film market as it is of any other.

Certainly the formulaic approach is still working, and films like *Total Recall* and *Die Hard* can still generate significant box office revenues. But perhaps they are not working quite as well as they did. To quote a recent edition of *Empire*, 'the action blockbusters have barely touched last year's box office, and one would-be blockbuster after another has opened well only to fizzle out after a few weeks'.[17] Consequently, the two most expensive films of the year were beaten to the top grossing spots on both sides of the Atlantic by the relatively low-budget *Ghost* and *Pretty Woman*.

Yet the industry seems to be slow to learn its lessons and, still desperately clinging to usually internalised and inherited audience images which simply may no longer accurately reflect the movie audience, is relying on existing formulas combined with bigger production and promotional budgets. As the American editor of *Empire* suggests, 'It seems, however, as if the runaway success stories such as the *Turtles*, *Ghost* and *Pretty Woman* are being regarded as little more than flukes, with unheard of millions still being shelled out on variations of old formulas'.[18]

For the film industry in general the bottom line is that consumers constantly change. An unquestioning reliance on well-established, apparently valid, but (with a changing environment) potentially inaccurate sets of audience images can therefore prove fatal for a film, a film company and perhaps eventually the film industry itself.

Marketing demands that the accuracy and relevancy of an audience image be tested empirically and explicitly before it is allowed to play a role in the decision-making process associated with film-making. It is not enough merely to pre-test the film once it has been made, when most of the production budget has been spent, and only a limited amount of product modification is possible. The analysis of the suitability of the product to the market must come at the earliest stages of the film-making process rather than the later if the British industry is not to waste its clearly limited resources. Further, marketing professes to offer the tools, techniques and models that will allow this type of research to be undertaken. An assessment of the appropriateness of these marketing techniques to the film industry in the analysis of audience images is one of the main aims of my research.

The fixed mind-set that this reliance on formulas creates is as evident in the British film industry as it is in the American, and I shall look at the implications of this in more detail in a later section.

Unquestionably, then, marketing does play a significant role in the film-making process, yet its explicit scope of effect is very limited, usually to the promotion of a film once it is ready for exhibition. It is also clear that this rather superficial manifestation of marketing is typical of industries that are production and sales orientated and have not yet explored the full scope of marketing.

What is the True Scope of Marketing?
This is a difficult question to answer simply. The discipline has been subject to a great deal of debate over the last twenty years. On the one hand we have those who see marketing as a relatively superficial add-on to the activities of a company, usually associated with promotional

which respond in similar ways to marketing stimuli. Our aims must then be to target specific segments for a particular concentration effort on our part.

These target segments are usually selected on the basis of which groups exhibit the greatest growth and profit potential, combined with which ones the company is best suited to serve on the basis of its past history, particular expertise and future growth plans.

How, then, do we design and tailor our offering, be it product or service, to suit the particular requirements and characteristics of our target segment? Marketing theory offers us an agenda of issues to be addressed, usually referred to as the *marketing mix*. At their broadest, the issues can be aggregated into four main groups, often referred to as the four Ps:

Product;
Price;
Place (distribution);
Promotion.

Each of these constituent parts of a company's offering to a market contains a host of subissues that must be addressed and questions we must ask if we are to be sure that our offering is suitable for our target market. These vary from the fundamentals of whether the product really satisfies the needs and wants of our customers in a better/cheaper/more efficient way than any competing products, to the details of whether our promotional medium suits the media habits of out target market.

This is where the third element of the core concepts of marketing, market research, plays a particularly vital role. Ultimately, this underpins all the activities already described. It is only through the generation, and use in decision-making, of accurate empirical data about our market that we can really be sure that our product actually has a market, and that we are tailoring it in a way that is valued and meaningful to our target segment.

The marketing concept goes further and emphasises the development of a flexible and dynamic market intelligence system which constantly monitors the business's environment for forces and events which might affect the market and the customers within it. Ultimately, then, a market-orientated company and industry attempts to develop a dialogue with the market it serves, a two-way flow of information which is designed to ensure that a company is always aware of what is happening in its market, and its market is constantly reminded of what it has to offer.

This all sounds a lot easier than it actually is, however, and the real

104

activities. On the other, there are those who tak
the marketing discipline, as typified by Drucker:
that it cannot be considered as a separate busines
view of the business seen from the point of view c
is, from the customer's point of view'.[19]

The scope, nature and implications of market
subject of much debate. Perhaps if we examine tl
ring themes and concepts in this debate we can be
what marketing is really all about, and suggest s
which the film industry might benefit if it more
marketing orientation. What, then, are the core tl
of marketing?

A Theoretical Overview

If we look at any major marketing textbook, or ind
plan, the following phrases are usually present:

- Consumer orientation.
- Marketing mix management.
- Market research and the generation, disseminatio
  market intelligence.

What, then, do these concepts describe, how do the
how are they manifested in a practical business envirc

In essence, they all find expression in a hierarchy c
strategies which forms the framework of modern mark
overly simplistic terms, the ultimate aim of marketing
most efficient and effective matching of customer ne
aspirations with company resources and capabilities.
by being consumer orientated, and manifesting this in o
decision-making.

How do we become *consumer orientated*? Firstly, by
fact that the consumer is the single most important e
company's business environment. Secondly, that the cu:
be the starting point when a company plans policy, strat
and thirdly, that the company does not, except in exce
sell its products to an entirely homogeneous market,
groups of customers buy the same product for often v
reasons.

Marketing theory goes on to tell us that we can ach
efficient, effective and, indeed, more profitable matcl
resources with customer requirements if we segment
geneous population into homogeneous groups which sl
characteristics, share common motivations for buying tl

process of marketing planning and implementation is infinitely more complex and involved than the process described above.

Marketing is not a cut-and-dried discipline. It is difficult if not impossible to definitively classify one company as being marketing orientated and another as not. It is more a matter of degree, the point being that marketing-orientated companies tend to think about customers and their needs more often, in a more structured way, with more information about them, and earlier in the planning process. For these companies, marketing is not seen as an add-on once a product has been produced, it is the forethought that goes into producing the right product in the first place.

Can Marketing Save the British Film Industry?

It is clear that the scope of marketing is much wider than that currently manifested in the film industry. Having established this, we are now in a much better position to assess the degree to which it can play a part in addressing the problems that currently beset the industry, and help to establish an environment in which sufficient domestic outlets for our indigenous talent are created and an economic infrastructure emerges to support them.

We must first establish the types of problems that the industry faces. This is not as easy as it sounds, however, as an inverse relationship has emerged between the number of British films being made and the number of explanations offered for the industry's plight.

The Problems

The majority of explanations have focused on structural issues. It has long been suggested that the divisions in the industry (whether they be the ever-widening gap between the independent and now almost non-existent studio sector, the divisions in the independent sector between production, distribution and exhibition or those within the workforce) are at the root of the British problem. It has also been suggested that we lack the mechanisms that would enable us to channel theatrical revenues back into the domestic industry. This has clearly become particularly significant with the demise of the Eady levy. As such, we are faced with a weak, fragmented and unstable production infrastructure.

For some the major problem is the lack of consistent government support for the industry. David Rose, former head of drama at Channel 4, suggests that 'I cannot think of another European country that gets less help from the government than we do',[20] or as veteran director John Schlesinger reveals, 'I'm astounded by the lack of support this government offers'.[21] Certainly, recent Budgets have done little to reassure those in the industry that its plight is high on the government's agenda. This lack of interest in the industry also extends to indigenous private investors, and we are therefore forced to look abroad for funding.

Others see the main limiting factor as Britain's apparently fragmented and frail film culture, both in terms of a visual culture that nurtures visually literate writers, and a popular culture among audiences that ensures a high level of interest in and debate about the medium. The proponents of the cultural approach are clearly also concerned about the abiding dominance of Hollywood, associated with the popularity of American films in the UK and the American stranglehold on distribution, and, with the advent of the multiplex, exhibition.

These are all self-evidently very significant constraints on the British film industry. There can be little doubt that they have all played a role in driving the industry into its present, rather sorry state. Yet it is also clear that these are relatively fixed constraints (at least in the short term), and rely on the actions of external agencies and groups to offer solutions.

It might even be suggested that addressing structural issues alone is not enough. The clear structural solution in terms of minimising the divisions in the industry must be the establishment of some form of British studio system. The most obvious way in which this might be accomplished is for more production companies to move into the distribution sector.

The precedent is certainly not good, however. We have only to look at the rise and rapid demise of the distribution company set up in 1978 by AFD/EMI to see the dangers of incurring the massive overheads of a national distribution company without an abundant supply of top-class *commercial* British films.

Recent events in America also point to the difficulties associated with smaller and middle-level production companies attempting to broaden their scope and move into the distribution sectors, competing directly against international majors who have entrenched relationships with the larger exhibition chains. It may indeed be the case that it is practically impossible to build a middle-level theatrical production/distribution organisation producing and marketing middle-budget films in the USA today. Is this the case in the UK?

A Change in Focus

Perhaps more importantly, we must also ask a fundamental question. Even if we do make more British films, and have the facility to distribute and screen them on a national and international scale, will people want to see them? This suggests a significant change in our focus from

106

a search for structural solutions, to a focus on the product (the film) and the procedures that are involved in its production.

This focus is reflected in a report by the BFI which suggested that, in the short term, the survival of the British film industry is dependent upon 'the ability of British films to seize a larger proportion of the market'.[22] This means, of course, people going to see British rather than American films in the national and international markets. In terms of the film product, can we compete with the Americans?

Bearing in mind the relative lack of commercial success of the majority of British films over the last twenty years our prospects do not appear good. Why is it, then, that British films have been relatively unsuccessful in the international market?

Clearly, there are as many explanations for this as there are reasons for the demise of the industry in general. Perhaps if we look at the type of film that has characterised most recent British film-making we can begin to get an idea of possible reasons for their lack of success.

A report by the BFI, looking at the relative success of the un-ashamedly uncommercial *Distant Voices, Still Lives*, voiced the following concern: 'films like these ... have become the only model for truly British film-making', but that 'it cannot serve as the universal archetype for British future contribution to world cinema'.[23]

This suggests that the British industry is very much production and sales led, that is, we tend to produce the product that we want to and hope that the public will like it, or can be persuaded to like it. As such, the film industry in the UK has come to resemble a very expensive hobby. Perhaps this is why director Stephen Frears proposes that, 'the British haven't got an eye for a commercial film'.[24]

Frears suggests that British producers and agents are unable to spot a commercial idea. The following quote from American screenwriter Michael Hauge perhaps implies that they are not even looking for commercial ideas:

In researching the British film industry to prepare for the London seminar, I asked one of the top screenwriting agents in England the following question: 'Let's say you had two original scripts come across your desk, and pretend the movies had never been made. One is *A Room with a View*, and the other *The Terminator*. Which one would you pursue?' His answer was, 'I'd probably pursue *A Room with a View* because that's the kind of movie I know the producers here are looking for.'[25]

If British producers and agents are asking their readers and story editors to find them another *Room with a View*, we must ask ourselves whether the British industry, with its apparent production orientation, is carving itself a niche or digging itself a grave in the international market.

Yet even if we are looking for commercial ideas, do we have the mechanisms in place to select them? How is new product development handled in the British film industry? According to a report by the BFI, in the UK 'script development is a particular weakness'.[26] The conclusion of the report is that, although there are a great number of scripts in circulation, most of them are unsuitable for development into feature films, and that ultimately the British industry lacks screenwriting talent and the visual culture to nurture it. Although this may be true, there are perhaps other variables which should be considered.

Certainly, the mechanisms by which film ideas are screened and selected deserve particular attention. I am sure we are all well aware of the use by producers of readers and the generation of 'coverage'. Ultimately, this is the first stage at which ideas for new films are screened for acceptability and potential. It is thus clearly a vital stage. As I am sure we are all also aware, however, these readers can be relatively inexperienced film school graduates, or the products of film industry nepotism, who have little experience of the film industry and even less of marketing and commerce. With the massive proliferation in the economic objectives associated with film-making they clearly have a difficult job in selecting the right scripts for development.

Unlike the executives of earlier years, their aim is not merely to find and develop a film product that will generate revenue in its first, second and subsequent waves of domestic theatrical release. Today, a film product, aimed at a mass market, must now not only have the appeal and 'legs' to be a success in the domestic theatrical market, its form and content must allow it to be exploitable in numerous other geographic and product markets. It must be easy to promote, have significant merchandising potential, be transferable and exploitable in the video sell-through and rental markets, suitable for TV syndication, and so on.

Thus the criteria for the evaluation and development of film projects have become more complex, intricate and involved, with inevitable implications for the decision-making process associated with the selection and development of scripts. Perhaps as an industry we should be asking how well our readers are being trained to look for commercial ideas. Are they caught up in the search for treatments, scripts and screenplays that fit into existing formulas? How significant is the role of the agent in putting together packages that short-circuit this system? How formal and structured is the process of idea screening and development? Perhaps most importantly, can the present approach be improved if a more marketing-orientated approach to

108

new product development is adopted? These are clearly very significant questions and are the major focus of my research.

The marketing approach to new product development is not designed merely to assist in finding new product offerings to exploit an already overexploited consumer. Rather, its aim is to provide a structured approach to developing new product ideas which assists in achieving the most efficient and effective match possible between customer requirements and company resources and capabilities.

The techniques used within this framework are designed to reduce risk and uncertainty at each stage of the new product development process, and ensure that we do not waste our resources in developing products that have no commercial potential. They are further designed to help tailor the product to the particular requirements of the target audience.

There are clearly limits to the extent of this risk reduction. The limit is perhaps, as Simonet suggests, 'the inability of respondents to predict reliably their own future actions'.[27] It may be, as Strick suggests, that there appears to be 'no simple consistent relationship between film themes, costs of production and box office receipts'.[28] Or it may be the case that, 'given the wide range of factors which can influence an audience to attend a movie at a given point in time, it is impossible to predict its actual performance in the market-place with consistent accuracy'.[29]

It is clearly impossible to completely reduce the risks associated with new product development, as no research can perfectly anticipate the nature of the demand for a product, but can we afford to give ourselves up to merely stirring box office tea-leaves? Adopting a consumer-orientated approach and utilising marketing's various tools and models can give a broad direction to a company's search for viable new products, and reduce an element of the risk of a mis-match.

New product development is only one of the areas in which marketing may have something to offer the British film industry; there are others. The role it plays in all of them is similar, however: the reduction of risk and uncertainty through the use of structured, empirically based and thoughtful analysis and planning techniques throughout all the stages of getting the film product to the final consumer.

For the British industry, marketing may thus have a particularly significant role to play. Any discipline which purports to reduce the risk associated with new product development, and aids in the development of commercial products, must surely help to attract indigenous investment back into the industry.

Again and again, we come back to the same point: the crucial element in the demand/supply equation is the product, the British film. Whatever British film-making distribution, or exhibition infrastructure does exist, it will only flourish if it produces sufficient numbers of the right films. These must be films that either have a potential international theatrical and auxiliary market large enough to attract a significant level of indigenous investment of funds (and which are successful enough to provide a sufficiently large return on this investment to encourage more), or films that are small enough, and targeted carefully enough into specific niche markets, to recoup their investment in a limited domestic and perhaps foreign release (or in auxiliary media).

Key Issues

It seems clear then that in the future the British industry cannot afford to rely solely on making the same type of films that have characterised most British film-making in the past, that is, low- to middle-budget, relatively uncommercial films that appear to be difficult to produce, difficult to distribute, difficult to exhibit, and sometimes rather difficult to watch. The British industry must broaden its scope, for in the future we may only have the luxury of making films like *Distant Voices, Still Lives* if we have first made such films as *Die Hard* and *Total Recall*.

What, then, are the key issues to be addressed for the British production company hoping to expand its scope and start making British films that are internationally successful? Ensuring that our films are commercial and exportable must begin, not with the early planning of an internationally appropriate and well-co-ordinated promotional campaign once a film is made, but rather with the selection of appropriate ideas for film projects, and their subsequent development. We must therefore examine the tools and techniques of marketing and assess the degree to which they can be used in the new product development process.

Clearly, positioning in the market, in terms of company scope and product, is vitally important. Again, marketing may be able to offer some useful analytical, planning and implementational tools for a company wishing to analyse its position in the market-place.

It might be suggested that, in producing films for the international market, the British industry has not only not learnt from its mistakes, but more importantly it has not learnt from its successes either. The success of a British film is often attributed rather vaguely to its 'Britishness'. What exactly does this describe? How is it manifested? Is it a quality worth developing in future films? How do we go about exploiting it? These are questions that marketing can help to answer.

The management of the product portfolio is another area that British companies must consider if they are to become more competitive and economically secure. It is noticeable that two of the more

110

significant British producers to emerge over the last ten years, Tim Bevan and Stephen Woolley, have both developed relatively clear, explicit and co-ordinated product policies for their companies, which have focused on specific target markets and the tailoring of products for those markets. Marketing offers a number of product portfolio models that can assist in the development of product strategies for individual films and groups of films.

Additionally, both producers appear to have a good idea of where their companies stand in the market in relation to their competition, and how they can use their particular capabilities and expertise to develop competitive strategies. It is essential that more British companies develop a greater sense of who they are, to whom they are selling their films (both in terms of customers and ultimate consumers), and how they can reach the market differently from other companies. Indeed, as Philip Dekom, a noted authority on the American film industry, suggests, 'there is no way to win without this kind of knowledge'.[30]

How is this knowledge to be obtained? I would maintain that marketing can offer some tools, techniques and concepts which may be useful.

The British film industry must investigate and assess the degree to which such tools can be used. It is clear that marketing has a role to play in addressing industry-wide structural and cultural issues, but for the individual companies in the industry this investigation must begin at the idea generation and development stage of film-making. It is only through the establishment of appropriate development mechanisms that the British industry will be able to break out of the *Room with a View* mind-set, and start developing films that are truly exportable and exploitable in the international commercial market.

Notes

1. Motion Picture Association of America, 1988 US Economic Review.
2. Barbara D. Boyle, 'Independent Distribution – New World Pictures', in Jason E. Squire (ed.), *The Movie Business Book* (London: Columbus, 1983).
3. J. Larmett, E. Savada and F. Schwartz, *Analysis and Conclusions of the Washington Task Force on the Motion Picture Industry* (Washington DC: US Government, 1978).
4. Geoffrey Nowell-Smith, 'Marketing and Sales: Interim report' (London: BFI, 1990).
5 Boyle, op. cit.
6. Suzanne M. Donahue, *American Film Distribution – The Changing Market* (Ann Arbor, Michigan: UMI Research Press, 1987).

7. Garth Jowett and James M. Linton, *Movies as Mass Communication* (London: Sage, 2nd edn. 1989).
8. Richard Kahn, 'Motion Picture Marketing', in Jason E. Squire (ed.), *The Movie Business Book* (London: Columbus, 1983).
9. John Strick, 'The economics of the motion picture industry: a review, *Philosophy of the Social Sciences* 8, December 1978.
10. Denis McQuail, 'Uncertainty about the audience and the organisation of mass communication', in P. Halmos (ed.) *The Sociology of Mass Media Communicators*, 'Sociological Review' Monograph 14, January 1969.
11. Herbert J. Gans, 'The creator-audience relationship in the mass media: an analysis of movie making', in Rosenburg and White (eds); *Mass Culture: The popular arts in America* (New York: Free Press, 1957), cited in Jowett and Linton, op. cit.
12. Thomas Simonet, *Performers' marquee values in relation to top grossing films*, Paper presented at the Society for Cinema Studies Conference, Temple University, Philadelphia, 1978, cited in Jowett and Linton, op. cit.
13. Jowett and Linton, op. cit.
14. Jowett and Linton, op. cit.
15. Gans, op. cit.
16. Jowett and Linton, op. cit.
17. Front Desk, *Empire*, September 1990.
18. Anne Thompson, 'Hollywood Shuffle', *Empire*, December 1990.
19. Peter F. Druker, *Management: Tasks, Responsibilities, Practices* (New York: Harper & Row, 1973).
20. David Rose, quoted in 'British Film, Where Now?', in *BFI Film and Television Handbook* 1991 (London: BFI, 1991).
21. John Schlesinger, quoted in 'British Film, Where Now?', in *BFI Film and Television Handbook* 1991 (London: BFI, 1991).
22. Geoffrey Nowell-Smith, 'But do we need it?' in Nick Roddick and Martyn Auty (eds), *British Cinema Now*, (London: BFI, 1985).
23. *BFI Film and Television Handbook* 1991 (London: BFI, 1991).
24. Stephen Frears, quoted in 'British Film, Where Now?', in *BFI Film and Television Handbook* 1991 (London: BFI, 1991).
25. Michael Hauge, *Writing Screenplays that Sell* (London: Elm Tree, 1989).
26. *BFI Film and Television Handbook* 1991 (London: BFI, 1991).
27. Simonet, op. cit.
28. Strick, op. cit.
29. Jowett and Linton, op. cit.
30. Philip Dekom, *There Ain't No Business In The Middle*, 1990 (Unpublished).

RESEARCHING THE MARKET FOR BRITISH FILMS

Geoffrey Nowell-Smith

This paper arises out of work conducted by the BFI on behalf of the British Screen Advisory Council in the spring and summer of 1990. The aim of the research was to establish a provisional profile of where the British film industry stood, and what its prospects were, in a period of increasing uncertainty. I was engaged in the part of the research relating to the market for British films, and for me at least the research opened up more questions than it answered.

As is well known, the Thatcher government's 1985 Films Act put an end to a system devised by Harold Wilson and a civil servant, Wilfred Eady, after the war. Under this system, British film production was supported by a levy on film exhibition. For the levy to work, there had to be audited reports from all cinemas to the Board of Trade giving full box office receipts and attendances at all programmes showing films entitled to reimbursement through the levy. The system was devised at a time when there was a certain continuity of British production, and money raised through the levy could be ploughed back into production entities which were ongoing. When the government introduced proposals to abolish the levy it was not just trying to put an end to a subsidy system of which it disapproved on market grounds; it was also recognising that the kind of British cinema the levy was designed to support no longer existed, and that there were no longer any rational criteria of redistribution. There was no case for milking exhibition, which was in a parlous state, with attendances dropping vertiginously and cinemas closing all over the place, in order to support a production sector that was no longer a national industry – being on the one hand no longer national but international and on the other hand no longer an industry as such.

The non-existence of British cinema in the traditional sense is a major question that nobody in the business seems to want to face up to, but which will have to be faced sooner or later if the relics of the industry are to do anything better than stagger from crisis to crisis. What concerns us here, however, is a lesser question, which is that,

113

when the levy went, so did the principal rationale for collecting statistics. A negative by-product of the otherwise quite sensible, in my view, legislation was that the Board of Trade (by now the Department of Trade and Industry) ceased to compile and issue statistics on cinema-going, making Britain the least well-informed country in Western Europe in terms of official statistics. The result is that we are now reliant for publicly available information on the voluntary reporting practised by the trade, selected results of which are published in *Screen International*. There is still a form of mandatory reporting, which is a matter of purely commercial practice. Exhibitors have to report to distributors and distributors have to report to producers on all matters affecting contractually agreed payments, so that, in theory at least, the producer of any film should know what the audience figures are which justify a particular payment. I am not sure how exhaustive these figures in fact are, and in any case they are not public information but confidential and only released when the interested parties wish to do so.

Meanwhile, over precisely the same period we have seen a further decline followed by a recent stabilising rise in cinema-going, accompanied by a massive increase in video viewing of feature films. Video viewing was not covered by official statistics and the figures we have for it are similar to those for cinema-going, namely, there is voluntary reporting of sales and rentals made public through the trade press, and in theory producers receive sales reports to back up their royalty payments. The published figures for video are even more fragmentary than for cinema and, of course, they only refer to legitimate trading in videograms: there are no figures for the undoubtedly large amount of semi-legitimate or outright illegitimate viewing of films on video.

The combination of these two major factors, the end of mandatory reporting to the Board of Trade and the rise of video as an alternative market outlet, means that basic information is hard to come by. This is a serious problem not just for people who like statistics but for the trade itself. It is extremely difficult to make intelligent business decisions on the basis of inadequate information.

One might think, then, that the trade would have acted (as would any other branch of business) to remedy the defect, and set up an alternative reporting system for the benefit of its members. The trouble is that 'the trade' in the relevant sense does not exist. There are the producers, the distributors, and the exhibitors, each of which is separately organised and each of which has separate (and possibly conflicting) interests to look after. British producers are interested in the market for their films, whether that market is home or export, in the cinemas, on video or on TV. The exhibitors are interested in product which fills their cinemas, regardless of where it comes from. The

114

distributors are interested in what they can sell, and since many of them are American owned they have no special interest in British product – more likely the reverse.

In the book trade, with which I am familiar, there are two major trade associations: the Publishers and the Booksellers. Since most of the market is for British books (or at least books which come out under a British imprint) there is relatively little conflict of interest and such conflict as there is certainly does not preclude co-operation on issuing statistics of interest to all branches of the business. Furthermore, this co-operation is traditional. In the case of the film trade, on the other hand, we have some rather inert trade bodies faced with a new situation and reacting to it in a generally negative and often suspicious way. The distributors' body, the SFD, is not opposed to introducing fuller published reporting, but it claims that there is opposition to this on the part of producers (particularly producers of unsuccessful movies) who are afraid that publishing abysmal results is bad for business confidence and could lead to a drying up of sources of investment. If this is true, it is a poor lookout for British production, because there is a limit to how long investors are willing to be conned. In the long term (and, indeed, in the fairly short term) both producers and their backers need to know very precisely which British films have done well and which have done badly, and, if possible, why. A certain tentative step forward was taken when the British Screen Advisory Council (BSAC), which represents all sides of the industry, asked the BFI to undertake the present research, but personally I am sceptical how much will come of it.

What do we need to know? Or, more to the point, who needs to know what? What information would be useful throughout the trade, and what would be of particular use to certain sectors or individuals? For example, if you were one of the following interested parties, what information would you like to have about the commercial past, present and future of the industry in Britain?

(a) A possible investor in a slate of films;
(b) An independent exhibitor;
(c) A technician wondering what your continuing career prospects in Britain were like;
(d) A member of staff in the BFI's information section.

Clearly each party would have the following particular needs:

(a) The investor would want to know which horses to back, which in practice probably means which producers have a proven record of success.
(b) The exhibitor would want to know something of how well films of

a particular type have played over the past few years, and what the effect of video hold-back, or competition from BSkyB, is likely to be on its theatrical prospects.

(c) The technician would want to know how many films are being made, with what crewing, and whether in five years' time there will be any onshore feature film production fully crewed in 35 mm.

(d) The BFI person would want to know all of the above and a lot more besides.

When I started this research there were many questions which were unclear to me regarding what information I was looking for, what information would be useful both in terms of my own research and other potentially interested parties (such as those listed above) and where to look to find it. While some of these remain unresolved, I think I now at least know what would constitute valuable information which would serve the needs of people with a variety of interests, from investors to technicians, to exhibitors, to people with a general informed curiosity about the state of the business (or even, dare I say it, the state of the art).

There are two broad areas of information in which I am primarily interested. First of all, I would want to know the gross turnover of the moving image business in this country, the amount of added value generated within the UK and the net balance between the UK and its trading partners. Within this I would want to know the proportion accounted for by British-made feature films.

Secondly, I would want to know more about the demography of moving image viewing, the amount of time that people spend in front of TV, video and cinema screens, and how much of this is spent watching British feature films and with what level of enjoyment (and for whom?).

The first of these initial, contextual questions is, I think, answerable with a reasonable degree of accuracy, at least in principle, though as far as I know it has never actually been asked. The second is at one level quite easily answerable, and a fair amount of research, ranging from BARB figures to the cinema advertisers' audience research (CAVIAR) to the BFI's *One Day in the Life of Television*, exists to provide the answer. However, what one really wants to have answers to – what is the importance of British films in contemporary cultural life? – is probably not answerable at all in quantitative terms.

Having established the context, I would then turn my attention to the question of earnings. At one time this was a simple question to answer. There were three markets: domestic theatrical, export, and subsidiary. Domestic theatrical was reported to the Board of Trade; from the gross box office it was not difficult to compute the return to the producer. Export earnings were also known to the government. Subsidiary markets, such as 16-mm non-theatrical and merchandising, were not very important. That was before broadcast television and video (both rental and sell-through) became such crucial markets for feature films. The small screen now amounts for more revenue returned to producers than the large screen, though how much more is anyone's guess.

On the theatrical side, the structure of contracts became more complicated and variable. It is no longer easy to deduce from the gross what the cinema take is, what the distributor's cut is, what are costs off the top, and how much is returned to the producer.

Video deals are even more complicated and variable; percentages are negotiated from film to film, and a gross of (say) £1 million may mean a net of £100,000 or nothing at all. Export information, as far as I know, does not have to be notified to the government, and in any case selling for export is even more complicated than selling in the domestic market. Producers generally find out after a while what the net export earnings of their films have been in various market areas, but they are unlikely to know (or to care), by the time the cheque comes in, what audience figures the net earnings represent. Furthermore, sometimes a customer is an investor or vice versa, and a 'sale' in a particular market may not be accountable as a sale at all because the market in question was presold as part of the initial investment package.

If, by way of a hypothetical example, Ruritanian Television puts money into a film, this could be a prepayment just for a licence to show the film in Ruritania or for a whole package of rights – theatrical, non-theatrical, pay-TV, home video – for Ruritania and the surrounding Greater Ruritania Prosperity Sphere; it might be a fixed prepayment or an advance on royalties; it might even be advanced as part of the equity; depending on how creative your accountants are, it might appear in a number of different places on the balance sheet.

If I can summarise the major points:

– gross income is only a very approximate guide to net income;
– net income is only a very approximate indicator of the size of the market a film has reached.

Now it is arguable that only a small proportion of the potentially available information is likely to be of interest to any particular sector, and that only the figures that are of direct commercial relevance to interested parties are worth researching. However, I would argue that all the data is potentially relevant, and for a variety of purposes. It is useful to know the size of the export audience, and not just the sums

117

remitted to British rights-holders under whatever deal happened to be in operation, while net figures are, of course, crucial to the viability of the production sector as such.

Moreover, a number of crucial policy decisions hinge precisely on the relation of gross to net. If we are concerned with the export performance of British films, we need to know both whether the films are reaching the market and whether the means by which they reach it is cost-effective. It is no comfort to the producer to know that a film opened on twenty-seven screens simultaneously in Freedonia or had an audience of five million on Rurisat 3 if all the earnings from exploitation of the film's success were skimmed off by middle persons of various kinds. One of the ideas being discussed in the Downing Street Seminars is the creation of an export agency similar to Unifrance or Unitalia; the operative question here is not only the potential gross – can British films be pushed out into wider markets? – but percentages – can the agency ensure that a better percentage of the profits are retained by the UK rights-holder?

Similarly for video. Both the quantity of video viewing and the structure of the royalty payments are of interest, and my suspicion here is that the marketing of British movies on video is hampered by a belief that it is not a real moneymaking market but something that brings in a useful trickle of royalties after the main markets have been exploited.

This leads on to the question of marketing costs. These are very considerable, and the bulk of them are usually incurred in connection with West End release and budgeted under that heading. This has a distorting effect on the producer's net figures for a film and leads to the rule-of-thumb assumption that theatrical release is where you try to recoup your costs and other markets are where you hope later to get your profit. However, if video and TV are also the source of your initial finance they are also part of the cost equation and should be treated as such. If these small-screen markets also need to be exploited it seems perverse to hope that a single launch will be sufficient for the product and to lumber the costs of this launch against one form of release only. The experience of book marketing is relevant here. Some books never make it out of hardback, some are paperback from the beginning, and some are simultaneously released in both formats. But the big popular successes are usually first published in hardback and then released in a cheaper paperback format, by the same or another publisher. The launch of the paperback does not generate many new reviews, but the marketing to the trade and general public is a large operation, separately budgeted. It is true that a book makes its reputation in hardback and that its promotion in that form generates spin-offs in the form of sales of subsidiary rights, paperback rights, and so

118

on, but this is never taken for granted. The paperback relaunch is an event in its own right.

To return to the question of statistics. There are three types of figures that one would ideally like to have:

(a) audience;
(b) money grosses;
(c) net returns.

You cannot always have all three types of figures for all types of market. For example, video rental figures do not tell you how many people watched the video. Moreover, net figures are often a commercial secret into which it is useless to try to pry. Grosses are generally obtainable, however, or could be made obtainable. With a bit of goodwill on all sides, it should be possible to put together sets of unit and money figures for theatrical and non-theatrical releases, video rentals and sales in export as well as domestic markets – similarly for pay-TV, if it happens. For other forms of TV, money figures may be hard to get, but audience figures can usually be obtained.

It would also be useful if information relating to the actual structure of deals was more often a part of public domain information. Grosses never tell you what a film makes for its original producer unless the structure is known, not to mention the distribution costs and who has borne them. The profitability of a film is therefore more often a matter of speculation than hard knowledge.

Finally, suppose we had all this information, what use will it be? Every armchair strategist will have his or her own ideas. What I should like to see is, on the one hand, a final knockdown blow for the illusion that 'British cinema' can make it in the big league, and on the other hand, a great deal of useful guidance on how British films can make it in the little league: low budgets, targeted marketing, and a non-Titanic sense of purpose. Maybe this, too, is an illusion. But it needs to be explored – preferably with something resembling a map.